Voodoo

Fact or Fiction?

Other books in the Fact or Fiction? series:

Voodoo

Fact or Fiction?

Kelly Wand, *Book Editor*

Bruce Glassman, *Vice President*
Bonnie Szumski, *Publisher*
Helen Cothran, *Managing Editor*

OPPOSING
VIEWPOINTS®
SERIES

GREENHAVEN
PRESS®

THOMSON

————— ✦ —————™

GALE

299.675
VOO

San Diego • Detroit • New York • San Francisco • Cleveland
New Haven, Conn. • Waterville, Maine • London • Munich

LIBRARY OF CONGRESS CATALOGING-IN-PUBLICATION DATA
Voodoo / Kelly Wand, book editor.
p. cm. — (Fact or fiction?)
Includes bibliographical references and index.
ISBN 0-7377-1314-3 (lib. : alk. paper)
1. Voodooism. I. Wand, Kelly. II. Fact or fiction? (Greenhaven Press)
BL2490.V66   2004
299.6'75—dc22   2003061228

Printed in the United States of America

Contents

Foreword

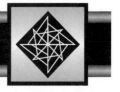

"There are more things in heaven and earth, Horatio, than are dreamt of in your philosophy."
—William Shakespeare, *Hamlet*

"Extraordinary claims require extraordinary evidence."
—Carl Sagan, *The Demon-Haunted World*

Almost every one of us has experienced something that we thought seemed mysterious and unexplainable. For example, have you ever known that someone was going to call you just before the phone rang? Or perhaps you have had a dream about something that later came true. Some people think these occurrences are signs of the paranormal. Others explain them as merely coincidence.

As the examples above show, mysteries of the paranormal ("beyond the normal") are common. For example, most towns have at least one place where inhabitants believe ghosts live. People report seeing strange lights in the sky that they believe are the spaceships of visitors from other planets. And scientists have been working for decades to discover the truth about sightings of mysterious creatures like Bigfoot and the Loch Ness monster.

There are also mysteries of magic and miracles. The two often share a connection. Many forms of magical belief are tied to religious belief. For example, many of the rituals and beliefs of the voodoo religion are viewed by outsiders as magical practices. These include such things as the alleged Haitian voodoo practice of turning people into zombies (the walking dead).

There are mysteries of history—events and places that have been recorded in history but that we still have questions about today. For example, was the great King Arthur a real king or merely a legend? How, exactly, were the pyramids built? Historians continue to seek the answers to these questions.

Then, of course, there are mysteries of science. One such mystery is how humanity began. Although most scientists agree that it was through the long, slow process of evolution, not all scientists agree that indisputable proof has been found.

Subjects like these are fascinating, in part because we do not know the whole truth about them. They are mysteries. And they are controversial—people hold very strong and opposing views about them.

How we go about sifting through information on such topics is the subject of every book in the Greenhaven Press series Fact or Fiction? Each anthology includes articles that present the main ideas favoring and challenging a given topic. The editor collects such material from a variety of sources, including scientific research, eyewitness accounts, and government reports. In addition, a final chapter gives readers tools to analyze the articles they read. With these tools, readers can sift through the information presented in the articles by applying the methods of hypothetical reasoning. Examining these topics in this way adds a unique aspect to the Fact or Fiction? series. Hypothetical reasoning can be applied to any topic to allow a reader to become more analytical about the material he or she encounters. While such reasoning may not solve the mystery of who is right or who is wrong, it can help the reader separate valid from invalid evidence relating to all topics and can be especially helpful in analyzing material where people disagree.

Introduction

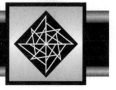

In 1927 journalist William B. Seabrook went to live in the jungles of Haiti, an island in the Caribbean, where he stayed with the family of a voodoo priestess who had agreed to instruct him in the island's religious customs. One day, Polynice, a Haitian farmer who lived on the island of La Gonave, took him in the broad daylight of afternoon to distant cane fields, where he had promised to show Seabrook authentic Haitian zombies, the walking dead. Seabrook wrote:

> They were plodding like brutes. The eyes were the worst. It was not my imagination. They were in truth like the eyes of a dead man, not blind, but staring, unfocused, unseeing. The whole face, for that matter, was bad enough. It was vacant, as if there was nothing behind it. . . . For the flash of a second I had a sickening, almost panicky lapse in which I thought, or rather felt, "Great God, maybe this stuff is really true.". . . Then suddenly I remembered—and my mind seized the memory as a man sinking in water clutches a solid plank— the face of a dog I had once seen in the histological laboratory at Columbia. Its entire front brain had been removed in an experimental operation weeks before; it moved about, it was alive, but its eyes were like the eyes I now saw staring.[1]

The Origins of Voodoo

The people Seabrook saw were purportedly soulless human corpses taken from the grave and imbued by sorcery with a mechanical semblance of life. The creation of zombies is just one aspect of voodoo. Haitian voodoo is, in fact, a complex, optimistic religion founded on exploring the mystical relationship between human beings and the guiding forces of the universe, not unlike Buddhism or Christianity. Although voodoo is still practiced by most inhabitants of Haiti today, belief in voodoo stretches back over many years and miles to the belief systems of western Africa, especially the areas now known as Nigeria, Benin, and Togo, the home of the Yoruba. Between the sixteenth and eighteenth centuries, French and Spanish slave traders raided these lands, transporting many Yoruba to Haiti and other islands in the Caribbean. Gradually, the African religious traditions merged with the tenets of Catholicism forced on the Haitians by their French slave masters to produce new ideas and a new faith that came to be known as voodoo.

Practitioners of voodoo believe in a grand master deity called Mawu or Djo who presides far above human affairs. All human beings are animated by *loas*, various spirits with colorful personalities who have been appointed by the Grand Master to help people with their problems. In exchange for this help, *loas* require frequent ceremonies in their honor presided over by voodoo priests known as *houngans*.

The majority of Haitian spirits are considered beneficial. The few that are considered evil can be summoned through the use of sorcery and persuaded to wreak havoc. Such ceremonies are the province of *houngans* for hire who specialize in sorcery known as *bokors*. The dark methods and ingredients employed by *bokors* are deemed effective, but the *bokors* themselves are held in low esteem. Their services range from affecting the weather to capturing someone's *ti bon ange* (little good angel), the part of the soul where a person's identity resides, to creating zombies through black magic.

The Living Dead

According to the voodoo belief system to create a zombie a *bokor* first lays exotic poisons on the victim's doorstep. The magic seeps into the victim body through the soles of the feet. Presently the victim dies and is buried. Within three days, the *bokor* visits the cemetery, recites an incantation, and cries the victim's name several times. The person awakes as a zombie and, bereft of will or reason, is now forced to do the bidding of whoever paid the *bokor*. Their most common fate is to become slave labor on a plantation far from any area where the person might be recognized. Others are released to wander the countryside and die a second time of starvation.

Zombies have no memory of their former lives. One Haitian legend says that dabbing salt on the zombie's tongue will restore partial speech and memory, although the wisdom of doing so would depend on the previous relationship between the zombie and the person dispensing the salt. To become a zombie is to submit to a fate worse than death. Some Haitians take extreme preventive measures, going to such lengths as skewering the heart of a newly dead loved one with a knife or severing the head in the coffin. Belief in zombies runs strong among the Haitian populace, but few Haitians claim to have actually seen a zombie for themselves.

I Was a Celebrity Zombie

On April 30, 1962, a Haitian farmer named Clairvius Narcisse was admitted to a hospital complaining of body aches, fever, and overall weakness. His condition worsened, and two days later doctors pronounced Narcisse dead. He was buried on May 3 in the cemetery near his hometown of l'Estere.

In 1980, eighteen years later, Narcisse was discovered by his horrified sister Angelina wandering in the middle of town. Narcisse told her that he had been zombified by a *bokor* hired by their brother. After his burial, the *bokor* had dug him up, beaten him, and dragged him to a distant farm, where he had toiled as a field slave with other zombies for two years. One day, another zombie revived and killed the slave master, enabling them all to wander away. Gradually, Narcisse's memory had returned. Despite slurred speech and weak muscles, he was a zombie no longer but was afraid to return home for fear of more reprisals from his brother. Thus Narcisse had wandered across Haiti for sixteen years, finding employment as a migrant farmworker. Eventually, he heard that his brother had died, and had now come home.

The Narcisse case was so strange and sad it captured international media attention. Narcisse was grilled by investigators on events during his childhood that only he or close family members could know. All of Narcisse's answers were correct. Over two hundred l'Estere residents vowed he was the real Narcisse.

In the wake of this publicity, others came forward, claiming to have had similar experiences that had gone unreported. One of these was Nategette Joseph. According to family members, Nategette had died in 1966 after being injured in a land dispute. In 1980, ironically the same year as Narcisse's emergence, she was discovered like him wandering the streets but with no memory of the intervening years. Sympathetic family members took her in. Other cases followed the same pattern: confused, stupefied people thought long dead, telling disjointed tales of being pulled from the grave and sentenced to hard labor for faceless masters.

The Search for Zombie Powder

These cases drew interest from the scientific community, but they were backed up by little hard evidence. Researchers were skeptical that people could be brought back to life. Still, some reasoned, maybe there was some logical explanation for the zombie phenomenon. Could the so-called magical powders employed by the *bokor* contain a powerful drug which somehow slowed down the victim's body functions enough to make him or her appear dead? The victim, never dead to begin with, would be buried and later be dug up by the *bokor* and administered an antidote. The *bokor* would continue to keep the victim drugged into an unresisting stupor, keeping the victim a vegetative slave for as long as the dosages were maintained or until the person died.

The possible existence of such drugs galvanized the scientific community, especially Heinz Lehmann, a professor of psychiatry at McGill University in Montreal, Canada, and Nathan Kline, a New York psychiatrist. Not only would a drug that rendered a patient insensible to pain and harmlessly returned him to consciousness revolutionize modern surgery, reasoned Kline, it could also "provide a fascinating model for experiments in artificial hibernation."[2] The existence of such rare drugs had already been documented. One example was, curare, a paralyzing plant poison used by natives of the Amazon rain forest in South America from which D-tubocurarine, a powerful muscle relaxant, was developed.

In 1982 Lehmann and Kline conferred with Wade Davis, an ethnobotanist (one who studies how people of a certain culture make use of indigenous plants) finishing his degree at Harvard University. Davis agreed to travel to Haiti to search for the zombie poison. Once there, Davis came face-to-face with the difficulty of his task. Most Haitians refused even to talk about zombies. Gradually Davis ingratiated himself with local officials who helped him get into several voodoo ceremonies and introduced him to *houngans*. One of these *houngans* finally yielded a sample of zombie poison, claiming it was only one mixture used among many, all of which produced different effects and styles of "death" in the victim. Davis analyzed the concoction. He found it contained a number of toxic ingredients, including tetrodotoxin, a deadly poison secreted by the female puffer fish. The *houngan* also gave Davis information about the antidote that is fed to the victim after he or she is exhumed, claiming its principal ingredient was a drug derived from the tropical plant *datura stramonium*, known in the Caribbean as the "zombie's cucumber."

Davis's findings were widely challenged. Some scientists claimed that tetrodotoxin was too lethal in any amount to allow any revival of the victim later. Davis's rebuttal was that certain plants in the powder diluted the poison's toxicity. Other critics charged that Davis had not collected enough samples and that the authenticity of what few he had was suspect. Davis pointed out he had recognized the first batch of powder given him by another *houngan* as fake immediately, and that it had taken him nearly a year merely to get what information and authentic specimens he had acquired to date. Davis insisted the second sample had been independently verified by chemists at Columbia University and the University of Lausanne in France.

A Weapon of a Secret Society

Davis contended that the practice of zombification had emerged within secret societies of the eighteenth and nineteenth centuries. In the 1700s, during Haiti's colonial days as Saint Domingue, the French had used masses of slaves to work sugar and coffee plantations. The runaway slaves who managed to elude French pursuit fled deep into the jungle, raised crops, and became self-sufficient. Moreover, they became guerrilla fighters, raiding the plantations of their former masters and trying to free other slaves. The French called these guerrillas Maroons, and their numbers grew to over forty thousand by the late 1700s.

In 1791 the Maroons led a successful revolt against the French. Secret meetings and voodoo ceremonies were held all over the island, where the downfall of the French was plotted and celebrated. After several years of fighting, the island was liberated, and by 1803 Haiti was free of foreign domination. The revolutionary leaders who had driven out the French considered their former Maroon comrades a threat to their power and persecuted them, driving them even further into secrecy. Over the ensuing decades, these splinter cells evolved into secret societies known as the *bizango*, a name derived from the Bissago, a west African tribe. Baron Samedi, the guardian of the dead, became the most cherished deity. Oaths of secrecy passed from one generation to the next kept the mysteries of the *bizango* intact. Among these, according to Wade Davis, were the methods and ingredients needed to inflict the dreaded punishment of zombification. Too powerful even to be harassed by the official Haitian authorities, Davis argues, the *bizangos* continue to coexist today as a secretive shadow government to whom Haitians without recourse may turn for aid, be it zombie powder or straightforward poison.

Voodoo Possession

Another of voodoo's mysteries is the *houngan's* supposed ability to channel spirits. Advice from the *loas* is the most common goal of all voodoo rituals, and the *houngan* offers his body up as a receptacle through which people can interact with these spirits and possibly gain their assistance. On the surface, such an effect would seem easy to fake, yet even researchers who have been present at voodoo ceremonies are flummoxed by what they admit are physiological peculiarities. *Houngans* possessed by spirits exhibit unusual strength and an above-normal tolerance for pain. They also speak in a variety of voices completely different from their own.

In the early 1900s American and British researchers attempted to dismiss this voice change phenomenon as ventriloquism. They suggested another *houngan* did the actual talking, throwing his voice from the shadows of another room to make it appear that the possessed person mouthing the words was speaking. This theory, however, failed to account for how the priest could create so many different voices in sometimes rapid-fire succession. Nor did it explain the other phenomena.

Several psychologists, such as E. Fuller Torrey, have proposed that possession is accomplished not through trickery but by the power of suggestion. In this mental process, a person believes so strongly in an idea that it becomes real to him or her. According to Torrey, the priest undergoing possession is so convinced that a spirit has entered his body that the spirit really does take him over, in a form of self-hypnosis. The person enters a trance and assumes the role of the spirit based on the personality details already agreed upon in Haitian culture. Everyone present at the ritual knows Ogoun is a brash, aggressive male spirit, so the *houngan* would act overtly swaggering. The *houngan* is not aware of his actions, Torrey emphasizes, but has created the Ogoun character completely from his or her own imagination.

Such industriousness on the part of the human mind is well documented, argues Torrey. Multiple personality disorder is a rare and serious form of mental illness that has been ascribed to demonic or divine possession for centuries. The same processes may very well be at work in voodoo ceremonies, he concludes.

White and Black Magic
Soon after Louisiana became a U.S. territory in 1803, many immigrants from Haiti traveled to New Orleans, bringing assorted voodoo practices with them. Over the course of the 1800s, this mishmash evolved into what became known as New Orleans voodoo.

New Orleans voodoo was characterized by more showmanship than Haitian voodoo and an emphasis on women as keepers of the religion. The most famous of these was Marie Laveau, who reigned as the "voodoo queen" of New Orleans for most of the mid-1800s. Laveau was both hated and feared, and she was central to many unexplained occurrences and controversies.

Another aspect of New Orleans voodoo was that magic, both good and evil, was considered part of mainstream voodoo. In Haiti, buying magical services for money seemed socially unacceptable at best. In New Orleans, voodoo was regarded as exotic and glamorous. Magic used for constructive effects, like healing or good luck charms, became known as white magic. Magic that brought injury or death to someone came to be known as black magic. In New Orleans, white magic was by far more prevalent than black magic.

One of the most significant symbols in white magic was the juju, or good luck charm. Jujus came in many varieties, some intended to be worn around the neck, others carried in a pocket or kept under a mattress. The majority of these were the feet of chicken and rabbits or the paws of monkeys. Others were even simpler, such as a straw broom that, when nailed over a door, was supposed to help ward off disease. Similarly, a horseshoe or alligator head hung over the door allegedly brought good luck.

Black magic took the form of bad luck hexes, also called mojos. According to followers of voodoo, mojos could be used to frighten people, make them ill, or even kill them. Mojo spells were sometimes accompanied by sinister trappings, such as a tiny black coffin on the victim's doorstep or a voodoo doll that could be pierced with pins, that represented the misfortunes to come.

Does Black Magic Work?
Voodoo queens and *houngans* obviously commanded the greatest respect among voodoo followers, but according to

most schools of thought, the magic would work for anyone who knew the right spell chants and possessed the proper materials. Many of these materials, as Wade Davis learned, were hard to come by, ranging from rare herbs and animal parts to human bones and soil or minerals from inaccessible areas. Generally, priests kept their collections of such artifacts cached in a small bag known as gris-gris, a French term meaning "gray-gray" (symbolizing the fact that anything concocted from the bag's contents might be used for either white or black magic).

Can black magic hexes actually work? Can voodoo priests use magic to make people die or go insane? One such case attracted widespread attention. In the 1850s New Orleans businessman J.B. Langrast publicly ridiculed the legendary voodoo queen Marie Laveau and accused her of orchestrating several robberies and murders with the aid of her followers. Shortly, gris-gris festooned with roosters' heads started appearing on Langrast's doorstep. Langrast's mood deteriorated until he eventually blasted his porch with a shotgun and fled New Orleans, leaving relatives and a sizable fortune behind.

Followers of voodoo would claim that Marie Laveau caused Langrast to go berserk by having a *loa* infect him with madness channeled through the gris-gris. Skeptics insist no proof existed Langrast was even insane, or even if he was insane, perhaps the madness was prompted solely by stress and fear of being killed by Laveau's followers. Psychologists like E. Fuller Torrey say the answer is obvious: Langrast's own mind damaged itself with the power of suggestion. Even though he claimed not to believe in voodoo, his subconscious, or inner mind, felt certain such magic might be possible. Psychologists believe that the power of suggestion can be intense enough to be fatal. If a victim accepts the firm belief that he is going to die from a curse, and his relatives treat the person as if he or she is already dead, the victim may very well die from the combined despair, depression, and neglect.

There is no way to know for sure whether voodoo black magic is the result of the power of suggestion, the result of a powerful *loa*, or some other cause. Only one instance of the inexplicable is enough to satisfy a believer; no amount can convince a skeptic. The unexplained feats attributed to Marie Laveau alone would fill at least as many volumes as the published efforts to debunk them.

The Second Sight

Another brand of voodoo that became popular in the United States is Santeria. Santeria, more in keeping with Haitian voodoo than the New Orleans style, revolves heavily around the worship of spirits. Those who believe in Santeria used the Yoruba word *orisha* to describe the spirits.

Practitioners of Santeria claim they can tell the future. According to believers, a *houngan* can sometimes acquire the gift of prophecy when possessed by an orisha. Generally, these predictions involve the people in the community and upcoming births, marriages, ailments, and deaths.

In one documented case from the 1970s, anthropologist Migene Gonzalez-Whippler attended a Santeria ceremony at which the celebrants sacrificed and ate a chicken. They did this, according to the priest, to protect Gonzalez-Whippler from impending danger. Now, they said, an orisha protected her. A few weeks later, Gonzalez-Whippler was flying in a plane from Denmark to the United States when suddenly the plane suffered serious engine trouble and was forced to turn back. Luckily, the plane landed safely. Gonzalez-Whippler and followers of Santeria believe that the orisha was responsible for her survival. Skeptics claim that the mechanical failure was nothing more than coincidence.

A Reality Based on Faith

Although many scientific arguments seek to explain away the mysteries of voodoo, its followers accept such supernatural elements as magic, hexes, and spirit possession as part of their daily existence. Skeptics claim no evidence exists to support the existence of a spirit world. Believers of voodoo see mountains of evidence everywhere that science deliberately chooses to ignore. To skeptics of voodoo, the history of man is a steady drumbeat of scientific progress gradually eroding the shackles of primitive superstitions as advances in technology and medicine render them obsolete. Yet there is a great deal about the human mind alone that science finds hard to explain. And even if science explained away every mystery of voodoo, many of its followers would not care. To them religion has always been a matter of faith, rather than evidence.

Notes

1. William B. Seabrook, *The Magic Island*. New York: Paragon House, 1989, p. 101.
2. Quoted in John Cossemann, "Voodoo: A Scientific Inquiry," *FATE*, September 1984, p. 42.

Chapter 1

Fact or Fiction?

The Power of Voodoo Is Real

Marie Laveau: Voodoo Queen of New Orleans

Raymond J. Martinez

If voodoo has a human figurehead in the United States, Marie Laveau, who reigned as New Orleans's flamboyant "Queen Mother" of Haitian sorcery for much of the nineteenth century, is undoubtedly it. Raymond J. Martinez, from whose biography of Marie the following piece is excerpted, paints a portrait of an uneducated but charismatic, business-savvy woman who established a track record for precognition during her early days as a hairdresser. She rose to eminence as one of the city's most visible and popular celebrities, all on the basis of her success rate at fortune-telling and "spells for hire"—both benevolent and malign. Martinez suggests no gifts short of true telepathy would have given Marie the edge or long-term clout necessary to dominate her competition and acquire the reputation that has only continued expanding ever since her death in 1881. Martinez's other works include *The Story of the River Front,*

Raymond J. Martinez, *Mysterious Marie Laveau: Voodoo Queen and Folk Tales Along the Mississippi.* New Orleans: Hope Publications, 1956.

The Immortal Margaret Haughery, and *Rousseau: The Last Days of Spanish New Orleans.*

Glendower: *I can call spirits from the vasty deep.*
Hotspur: *Why, so can I, or so can any man;*
            But will they come when you do call for them?
                        Shakespeare—Act III, King Henry IV

Had Marie Laveau been Glendower she could have answered Hotspur. "Yes, they come when I do call for them," and Hotspur would have believed her, just as thousands of prominent men and women of New Orleans believed whatever she said; they wanted to believe; they dared not disbelieve, for she had the power to scare the wits out of them. How she acquired this power is a subject that has never been explored. Seeing is believing, and when people were confronted with evidence that she could "make their wishes come true," and tell them what to do to bring themselves good luck, such as wearing good luck charms, usually the end of a black cat's tail or a rabbit's foot or a twig or pebble from a graveyard, or any other item which she sold, thousands flocked to her. Why not? She was actually wonderful. She had been instrumental in causing the election of politicians to high offices; she had relieved the misery of many who had loved and lost and were pining away—suddenly there came a change and they found themselves loved in return—she had destroyed enemies or brought them bad luck; she had performed other miracles which astonished the people. How did she do this? Was it through power she gained from the help of evil and good spirits alike or was she a common sorcerer who hurt one for the benefit of another? These are questions yet unanswered.

Marie Laveau was, from all accounts, an ignorant woman.

If she could read and write that was the extent of her education. It is certain that she never read a book in her lifetime, and doubtful that she ever read a newspaper. Yet men and women who had been educated at the leading colleges and universities of the United States and Europe went to seek her advice, not only in personal matters, but in matters of political activities concerning the local government and the nations of the world. There were among her clients, of course, also the lowly, who had none but personal interests, and they were in the majority.

The records of vital statistics show that Marie Laveau, a free mulatto, was born at New Orleans in 1794, and married Jacques Paris, a carpenter, on August 4, 1819. The marriage was performed by Pere Antoine, who recorded the couple as free persons of color. She claimed, according to her daughter, "Mme." Alexandre, that the Laveaus were descended from the noblest blood of France. This may or may not have been true; but it was possible, of course, for it would not have been strange for a person with Marie Laveau's keen intelligence to have ancestors of more than average ability. . . .

She and Jacques Paris, who is reported to have been three-fourths white, made their residence at what is now the 1900 block of North Rampart Street, in a house which her father, Charles Laveau, gave them. They led a normal and respectable life, and although they may have attended Voodoo meetings they were not themselves practicing that cult. There was no issue from this marriage. It is said that Jacques left Marie a short time after the marriage, but this is doubtful, for she was a beautiful woman, intelligent, and capable of holding any man—if she wished to. She may have "given her husband the gate." Who knows? But it is certain that Jacques died in 1822, less than three years after the marriage, and Marie assumed the title of "Veuve (widow) Paris," which is noted in the inscription on her tomb in the St. Louis Cemetery No. 1. There is no record of the interment of Jacques Paris. If he left Marie, as some say, he may have gone back to Santo Domingo, from whence he came. The fact that there is no record of his interment, but merely the statement that he died, lends credence to the rumor that he had deserted Marie for had he died in New Orleans and while living with her there would have been a record.

Marie and M. Edouard

Marie first began to consider Voodooism as a profession when, about 1826, she offered her services as hairdresser to the elite ladies of New Orleans. While rendering this "personal" service she found many women willing to "let their hair down," as the expression goes, and they told her of their hopes and disappointments.

For instance, she would say, "Ah, Mademoiselle, you look sad—and why?"

"Why? I will tell you why."

"You don't have to tell me; I know."

"How can you know, Marie? I've never told a soul, not even my mother."

"Yes, I know that; but you don't have to tell me; I know. It's M. Edouard. He was supposed to take Mademoiselle Regina out tonight."

"Tonight! How do you know all that?" . . .

"Mademoiselle, you have pretty hair."

"Don't tell me that; I wish I didn't have any at all, I wish I were dead, that's what I wish."

"You are pretty, Mademoiselle—you are good; you deserve a good man."

"I told you not to say that."

Marie twisted her body with the suppleness of a snake, then made passes in the air, and knelt at Mademoiselle's feet. "I can stop him from seeing her."

"You can stop him? What do you mean? You mean you can stop him from seeing her tonight? Is that what you mean?"

"Yes, Mademoiselle."

"How?"

"When I pass his house tonight I'll put gris gris [a mixture of herbs and other ingredients with supposedly magical properties] on his doorstep, and there will be a change, a big change. You will see."

"I've heard that you can do things like that."

"Yes. That will cost you twenty-five cents—for the gris gris."

"Twenty-five cents! I'll give you five dollars if you can do it."

"Give me twenty-five cents, and if I succeed you can give me the five dollars the next time I come."

"No, I'll not do that; I'll give you the five dollars for trying—and if you succeed, Marie, I'll give you ten."

"I will succeed."

"Then hurry and fix my hair. I want you to put the gris gris on his steps right away."

Marie hurried, but she gave Mademoiselle a very beautiful hair-do, and she was pleased. She wished that Edouard could see her now.

That night as she sat thinking that she had made a fool of herself giving that ignorant woman five dollars for something that she could not possibly accomplish, there came a knock at the door. The valet went to answer, and returned to announce M. Edouard.

Mademoiselle's heart stood still; she nearly swooned. "Show him in." She was afraid; she did not know what had happened; she did not wish anything bad to happen to Regina, as much as she disliked her, and she wondered if M. Edouard had come to tell her bad news, something terrible which the gris gris had brought about. She did not want M. Edouard now if the gris gris had forced him to come to her, and she was cool. But his manner reassured her; he wanted her, and that was why he came. He proposed marriage that very night, and they were married in a month.

She never told him about Marie, but she went to her and gave a good sum of money, not only for what she did, but as a bribe not to mention it ever. How did Marie do this? Mademoiselle did not ask. But Marie volunteered: "I knew it would be so; I put the gris gris. That's where it came from, from the High Heavens. Because it was right.". . .

Telepathy

Telepathy, whose limits no one can define at present, can filch knowledge subliminally and systematically from living people at pleasure. So says Dr. James H. Hyslop, formerly Professor of Ethics in Columbia University in his book PSYCHICAL RESEARCH AND THE RESURRECTION. "There are growing signs that a new world of facts promises to open to human vision and interest, and only self-complacent dogmatists any longer ridicule the subject." Telepathy is not a new experience or idea; it was known to the ancients. It is reported that when Caesar was in Gaul with his army a rumor was circulated in Rome that on a certain date, five weeks hence, he would arrive with 3000 prisoners he had captured. The people were jubilant. The Senate began to make preparations for a welcome, and a Roman Holiday gave rise to wonder among the inhabitants of Mars as to what was happening on the little planet called the earth. But there was a member of the Roman Senate, such as we have in Washington, who liked to investigate everything, and he recommended that a committee be appointed to inquire where this news originated. Nobody could tell. Nobody knew. It would have been impossible for Caesar to have communicated this news to Rome within a day. The swiftest messenger could not have made the trip inside of three weeks. An old woman, like Marie Laveau, had received the message via telepathy, and had told somebody who spread the news. When she heard of the Senate's purpose to investigate she either killed herself or fled the country. She may have gone to Greece and lived under another name, forever in fear. The Senate's committee reported that the rumor was a pure falsehood. But on the date specified Caesar arrived with his 3000 prisoners. Rome was amazed. The Senate appointed a second committee to investigate the first.

Marie Laveau knew nothing of mental telepathy. If her mind instantly communicated with M. Edouard's and she read his thoughts—that he had made up his mind to marry Mademoiselle—she attributed the flash of knowledge to the High Heavens or to the gris gris. The truth is that somehow, she knew not how, she became suddenly aware of what M. Edouard was going to do.

She could have gambled in her foretelling and in her promises, and taken the chance that she would win. But her average of winnings was too high. She must have had some means of knowing. . . .

Marie Laveau Embraces the Cult, Voodooism

Marie Laveau became so popular among the young ladies of New Orleans, and the money which she received for her favors was so great an amount that she felt she could do even better in a professional way. She knew that Voodooism had become the rage of New Orleans. But she also knew that the Voodoos were devil worshippers, inclined to do harm rather than good. She was too clever to accept a cult in which there was only destruction, and no profit. Anyway, as she was aware, "The devil can cite Scripture for his purpose." She proceeded to change the very purpose of Voodooism; it was to become a profitable business which offered to satisfy the desires of the people; that is, to show how to procure the things dearest to their hearts, and for which they had long prayed. In this she was to succeed as no Voodoo Queen ever had. She was to keep the ritual, for showmanship was necessary. She knew that. There were to be the monster serpent lodging in the Alabaster box, the black cat and the rooster. Where she procured the Alabaster box is unknown. Some said that it was given her by Mommer, the chief deity of the religion, while she was still in the Congo. Other versions had it that the box was brought from Heaven. The great Zombie (as the snake was called) fed only upon fair and tender children. Serious mention of this was made in the Picayune of June 25, 1873. But Marie added to this unholy arrangement statues of saints, incense, and holy water.

These additions were the secrets of Marie Laveau's success; they were the media through which she wielded her power and authority. . . .

Marie's Ascent to Queenhood

There were several Voodoo queens complacently occupying their thrones when Marie decided that she was to reign alone. This precipitated a terrible battle for supremacy, nearly as bad as the War of the Spanish Succession, which lasted for several years. Marie conquered by fair means and foul. The former queens, now humbled, served under her. They had actually been subdued by her success, for she had among her clients many of the elite ladies of the city, for she knew them well (she had been their hairdresser), and there were gentlemen of prominent families who visited her. These gentlemen customarily had mulatto "mistresses" and mulatto children. Marie knew all about this, for these "mistresses" often consulted her. Obviously her claim to power did not come only from holy water and incense, but from an inside knowledge of the lives of certain ladies and gentlemen.

The Picayune of June 25, 1873 says that there were (at that time) three hundred Voodoos in the city, presided over by a queen, "and amongst whom are numbered, strange to relate, at least eight or ten white women who partake as the others in the hellish orgies. Outside of these 'firm ones' there are about a thousand more who, while ashamed to openly acknowledge their belief, secretly have faith, and can be found on the sly practicing its tenets. The belief is one of fear. . . ."

Marie formed a liaison with Captain Christophe Duminy Glapion about 1826. Since she did not marry him the date of their coming together is uncertain. She was then 32 years old, and more attractive than when she married Paris. Glapion was 37, and was also a free person of color. He was, it is said, a very handsome man. From this union, such as it was, there were fifteen children. He died on June 26, 1855, and was buried in the Laveau tomb in the St. Louis Cemetery No. 1. He was apparently a good man, and undoubtedly a good husband.

Glapion seems to have taken no part in the Voodoo rituals, for his name is never mentioned in the newspaper accounts of that cult. Why Marie did not make a god of him instead of the snake, Zombie, is somewhat surprising, for he rendered meritorious services in the War of 1812, having been a member of the Company of Men of San Domingo at the Battle of New Orleans. . . .

Dispensing Poetic Justice

Marie had by this time become quite famous. People went out of their way for a glimpse of her, for she was the great Voodoo Queen who could do wonders in good and bad; the greatest interest was, of course, in the bad things she could do; but any bad thing she did for one was good for another. . . .

This was her philosophy. When the parents of a very attractive young lady offered her a good sum of money to bring about their daughter's marriage to a wealthy Creole who had spent his youth in dissipation, and had no respect for women, she agreed to the bargain and succeeded. It is said that she got a mocking bird drunk and placed it in a cage outside the young lady's window. As the bird began to sing her heart went out to the wealthy Creole. But the mocking bird was never the same after that; it became a confirmed alcoholic, and had to be fed whiskey every day. The Creole led his wife a miserable life; like the mocking bird he became a confirmed drunkard, and was finally killed in a street brawl. His wife died shortly afterwards, and her parents inherited a good sum of money. These were the "sweet uses" Marie made of adversity, and the good she found in everything.

There was a young man of a very aristocratic family in New Orleans who had seriously "wronged" a beautiful and innocent girl of a lower but respectable social station. Her father had gone to the district attorney and charged him with rape, and the evidence which he produced was very convincing. The young man's father was greatly alarmed, for public sentiment seemed strongly in favor of the young lady, owing, no doubt, to her beauty and good reputation. Moreover, the attorney employed to defend his son seemed discouraged, and talked of settling for a light sentence. Finally, the young man, being informed of his predicament, went himself to see Marie Laveau, and pleaded for help on his bended knees. He offered her a good sum of money, which, he said, he was certain his father would provide. After hearing his story, which he related in great detail, she assured him that she would bring about his acquittal.

As the time for the trial approached the young man informed his father of his interview with Marie, and of his promise.

"Ha," said his father, "that is ridiculous. But if she succeeds I will give her the house that I own on St. Ann Street."

"I will tell her that, and she will hold you to it," said the young man.

"Very well, I always keep my word."

On the day of the trial Marie made a condiment of veg-etables having an agreeable odor, and placed it carefully in the right hand corner of the judge's desk. This she did about six o'clock in the morning when there were few persons about, and certainly none in the courthouse. She then placed a bag of powdered brick on the front steps of his residence, and on his front door she pinned a note which said: "The boy is innocent," and to this she had the effrontery to sign her name, believing that her influence would have weight.

The jury was composed of the play-boy type of men, most of whom had probably committed the same character of crime, but had not been brought to justice. The prosecut-ing attorney, was, however, a man who had risen from the ranks and knew the "wronged" girl very well. He, therefore, fought hard for conviction. "Mark well what I say," he cried; "if this man is set free, then none of our young girls are safe in this city, and that would be an unusual situation in this civilized world, for the laws and customs protecting women are ancient. Read your Bible." Marie wanted to speak. She had something in her mind. But she dared not. Instead, she flipped a small ball of paper, in which was wrapped a strand of her hair, up into the air, and it fell upon the prosecuting attorney's shoulder. He said no more, but left the matter to the jury.

The verdict rendered was "not guilty."

The stain upon the young man's name was, therefore, re-moved, and his father kept his promise, and gave Marie a house. This may have been the cottage at 152 St. Ann Street (now 1020) which was the residence of her numerous fam-ily until her death in 1881 at the age of 87. There is no clear record that it was or that it was not.

The young man, having been set free, went to church frequently to offer thanks for his good fortune. As time went on he brooded over his crime, and associated no longer with his former companions. He became very religious. Finally he sought the girl he had "wronged" and begged her to marry him. She refused. Again he went to Marie and asked her to help him win the girl, for he could not rest until she became his wife and had forgiven him. The Voodoo Queen, now at the height of her glory, told him to have no concern, the girl would marry him within a month. She proceeded to make a concoction of love powder (being ordinary talcum), feathers, pulverized lizard eggs, and the hair of a jackass, which she placed in a bag for him to wear around his waist. She then took strands of hair from various parts of his body and spread them upon the young lady's doorstep.

The girl continued to reject his advances. But one day as he was leaving church he met her just arriving to pray for her aunt who was ill. Upon seeing him she turned suddenly to run away, but stumbled and sprained her ankle. He rushed to her and picked her up gently, begging her to trust him to take her to a doctor and then to her home. She was so impressed by his gentleness and solicitude that she yielded, and the next moment he kissed her. The following day she limped to the altar with him. . . .

The Queen of Showmanship

Marie's rituals were, of course, so outrageously vulgar that children were forbidden to witness them, and the adults who attended went secretly, sometimes in disguise, for no person who pretended to be self-respecting could admit that so depraved a performance was enjoyable or even interesting. Marie was the central figure, and she dressed like a gypsy, with a bandana about her head, flashy rings on her fingers and ears, and gold bracelets on her wrists. Her dress was long and full, hanging gracefully from her shoulders. It was always of a dark color. Her eyes, large and brown, sparkled like emeralds against her dark skin. She was the picture of health and vigor. Were she here today in her youth or middle age some motion-picture producer would employ her—for oriental scenery if nothing else.

The ritual, which was held once a week, took place in the yard of her cottage on St. Ann Street, and began with her dancing with the snake (which she called Zombi) wrapped about her. It is said that this snake was 20 feet long and venomous. This is doubtful; it may have been 10 feet, and harmless; nine-tenths of all species of snakes are harmless. When she danced she never moved her feet, only her body, twisting it to the rhythm of the music. But since she was pregnant most of the time during a period of at least 25 years (if she had fifteen children) she probably omitted her dance at infrequent intervals.

After she had led the way, she sat down and gave instructions to her performers. They were men and young girls who danced practically in the nude, usually holding bottles of rum or whiskey from which they drank. Naturally they grew bolder and bolder as the night progressed, and finally indulged in rather intimate love-making in corners of the yard where darkness did not completely conceal them. Meantime the music played louder and louder, and the dancers grew wild; they trembled and shook from excitement; some of them swooned and had to be revived with cold water; others wept and prayed or sang religious songs—they were all hysterical. Many respectable and even prominent men and women of New Orleans attended these orgies. The police often appeared to make a pretense at raiding the place, but they stood in awe of Marie, and after a few words with her went away. After all, there was no law against dancing with a snake, or a fish, which some maintain was another of her dancing companions; there was no regulation against drinking tafia (which was then the drink of the town), nor against praying and singing. The noise was the only basis for complaint, and that was a minor offense. If the revelers drank blood, perhaps from swine, there could be no objection to that; it was good for them; it promoted health. If the police wanted some favor, such as gris gris, or a reading of their fortunes without charge, Marie was ready to accommodate them. . . .

Her St. John's Eve ceremony, which took place every year on June 23 at a point where Bayou St. John enters Lake Pontchartrain, was a gala affair that attracted the attention of the press, the public and the police. . . .

There were girls who danced in one-piece garments merely to appear indecent, for if the night was windy there was little of them concealed, or even if the night was calm the breeze which their dancing created left little to the imagination. The men wore loin cloths, the customary dress of the Negroes of Haiti, and, for that matter, South Africa and most tropical countries. In New Orleans when women wore hoop skirts and corsets and men wore stiff shirts and stocks about their necks, the loin cloth seemed indecent—but that is why the dancers wore it. There is an art in showmanship. But there is a deceptive simplicity in art. The grotesque performances of Marie Laveau may not have been entirely agreeable to her, for she is said to have been a very intelligent person, but she had to satisfy her audience. In this she succeeded above all her competitors, and became the central figure in the Voodoo world of New Orleans.

Music filled the air. There was the fiddler with a bottle of tafia beside him, and although he became blissfully and inoffensively drunk he played on through the night. There were also the huge drums made of crude material, all making as much noise as possible, perhaps driving the fish to the middle of the lake and disturbing people who lived miles away. The snake, Zombie, being deaf, was perhaps the only undisturbed creature in the vicinity.

Charms of luck and love-charms were on sale, and nearly every person who attended bought them. The proceeds from this show were sufficient to keep Marie in money for several months. What she did with her money is a mystery, for she lived always in a ramshackle cottage, and never seemed to be affluent. She had many children, but certainly did not send them to colleges, universities or finishing schools; and her husband, if he worked, must have been at least self-supporting. She was, in her way, charitable, and may have enjoyed helping people in need. It is known that she frequently nursed the sick without charge, and even attended yellow fever patients when nobody would go near them. Perhaps she knew, for many things were mysteriously revealed to her, that she was not to contract the fever. . . .

A Folk-Lore Figure

Much has been written about Marie Laveau, and she has become a figure in the folk-lore of New Orleans rather than a character of its authentic history. Her beauty and her abilities won the people's interest, and often their admiration in her role as the famous queen of the Voodoos. Confucius said; "I have not seen one who loves virtue as he does beauty." The newspapers of her time gave few of the specific incidents wherein she performed wonderful deeds for her clients. Such stories were handed down. The names of the persons who reaped amazing results from her gris gris and mind-reading have naturally been withheld (and no doubt forgotten); yet only they could have testified to the truth of what she claimed. Without any semblance of a date, the stories, perhaps changed many times in the telling, are quite remarkable and extremely interesting.

Voodoo Is a Gateway to a Parallel Universe

Reginald Crosley

On the surface, voodoo and quantum physics seem to have little in common. Reginald Crosley believes otherwise. In the following piece Crosley suggests a synthesis exists between African-Haitian spirituality and modern science. Voodoo, he says, is a metaphysical experience, a bridge to parallel universes and mystical dimensions, all confirmed by the tenets of quantum physics and discoveries of astronomy. Reginald Crosley is a physician specializing in internal medicine and nephrology and the author of *Immanences*, a book of poetry.

According to some new theories developed by subatomic physicists, we may be sharing our reality with another world made up of invisible intangible shadow matter or

Reginald Crosley, *The Vodou Quantum Leap: Alternate Realities, Power and Mysticism*. St. Paul, MN: Llewellyn Publications, 2000. Copyright © 2000 by Reginald Crosley. Reproduced by permission of the publisher.

dark matter operating in at least ten dimensions (March, *Science Year*, 184).

The idea of dark matter came to the forefront in 1930,

> when the Swiss-American Fritz Zwicky calculated that galaxies in large clusters were moving so fast that the gravity provided by their visible stars was insufficient to hold the galaxies together (Turner, *Science Year 1994*, 184).

His calculation brought forth the first inkling that there is much more matter in the cosmos than meets the eye. Scientists in the field now estimate that the unseen matter makes up about 90 percent or perhaps 99 percent of the universe mass (Turner 184).

The existence of the dark matter poses a challenge to the quantum theorist in that its existence is not a matter of choice, as far as the presence of the observer is concerned. The consciousness of the observer does not make it pop in or pop out of existence. It is a singularity in the reality of the universe. We know now that our universe is full of that shadow matter. Our very own Milky Way is full of it and we are unaware of it through our sense perception. We cannot see it because we see mainly by means of electromagnetism, and shadow matter does not emit light. Also, it is not detectable by radio telescopes, infrared, or x-ray instruments. Furthermore, shadow matter passes freely through ordinary matter, so that we cannot feel it like we feel ordinary objects that we touch. That reminds us of the ghosts that populate the imagination of the superstitious people. However, the presence of the dark matter is detectable by the gravitational effects it exerts in the galaxies of the universe. Large amounts of that invisible matter exert stronger gravitation forces than would be expected from the amount of matter visible in the stars, gas, and dust in the galaxies (March 194).

Now, the next big questions are: What is dark matter? What does dark matter consist of? We still don't know exactly what it is made of, but as usual, we have many theories. . . .

Some astronomers believe that shadow matter consists of dead stars, neutron stars or the celebrated black holes, the collapsed cores of dead stars, or balls of gas located mainly in the halos surrounding the galaxies. But as Stephen Hawking would say, "Black holes ain't that black," they emit something over the "event horizon" that can be picked up by our instruments. Furthermore, those bodies are made of ordinary matter that either gives off radiation in the form of light like stars do, reflects it like planets do, or absorbs it like dust does (Primack 1990, 120).

Some other astronomers believe that dark matter is something far more exotic, such as an unknown form of matter left over from the earliest moment of creation (Turner 1994, 184). They suspect that it is not made of atoms at all (Primack 120). Astronomers have surveyed the cosmos at all wavelengths of the electromagnetic spectrum and have been unable to find any radiation in the shadow matter halos. Thus, physicists have come to propose the existence of unknown new particles. . . .

The Shadow Universe

Considering that dark matter occupies 86 percent of the total density of the universe, while ordinary matter with all its variety and richness accounts only for 14 percent, there is plenty of room for an overabundance of alternate realities. The realm of dark matter should not be reduced to the presence of mass and gravity counteracting the expansion of the universe and leading eventually in a very distant future to the Big Crunch (Primack 123). The parallel universe of the shadow matter could include an abundant variety of sub-parallel worlds with living entities, existing in multiple dimensions as seen in the superstring theory, and responsible for many unexplained phenomena reported by psychics, seers, schizophrenics, and ordinary people such as appari-tion, materialization, dematerialization, metamorphosis, levitation, psychokinesis teletransportation, and ubiquity. These unexplained phenomena would be produced by the interactions of the shadow universe with our wave function or quantum dimension. At this point, we can postulate that all other reality or dimensions enter into interactions with our commonsense reality first through our quantum di-mension or wave function. In that regard, the realm of the vodouns, that alternate reality of the Haitian world vision, is rich in manifestations of these interactions.

Furthermore, considering the vast amount of dark matter in the universe and its presence in the Milky Way, our own galaxy, it won't be farfetched to imply of its very presence in the composition of everything on planet Earth, including *Homo sapiens* himself. The ancient Egyptians, and after them the Greeks and the Judeo-Christians, have always main-tained that the nature of mankind is tripartite with body, soul, and spirit. . . .

Shadow Entities

Vodou is an immaterial force existing everywhere.[1] For mod-ern parlance, it is a ubiquitous force, existing everywhere in space-time. This force can be actualized as space-time events—persons, objects, and physical matter such as urns, rocks, trees, or rivers. This force is not the product of simple imagination, like the Western world would like us to be-lieve, but is an essence of non-ordinary realities or alternate realities, manifestation of invisible matter, and/or quantum dimension of reality that the African intelligence and sensi-tivity have learned to harness and control.

The vodouns are spiritual entities, or shadow-matter enti-ties that have had a long commerce or interaction with hu-man beings. Some would be the shadow-matter component of the tripartite human beings. Some appear to be originally from a parallel universe and then have acquired novel characteristics from long interactions with mankind. Their manifestation on the sensory level of existence in our ordinary reality occurs in a sporadic manner most of the time. Some predisposing factors, rituals, and quantum connection must be produced or be in place to allow an irruption from shadow reality to ordinary reality. The houngan or Vodou priest, whose name means "master of the vodouns" (Métraux 327), is the one who has the knowledge to induce a manifestation or irruption in our ordinary reality as possession or channeling. This knowledge would be the equivalent of the science of an experimental physicist in possession of a supercollider-type of equipment capable of making manifest the existence of a boson or a fermion. The houngan makes manifest the shadow matter of the vodouns' reality. There seems to exist an attraction for the visible world on the part of the shadow world. The entities of the alternate reality crave for the joy, actions, and pleasures of ordinary reality. Thus, they enter into some association, connection, or covenant with earthlings in order to partake of the bounties of visible matter or ordinary, commonsense reality.

The initiates in the mystery of Vodou see the entities as diversely oriented forces that we must harness to dominate nature or to use for good or evil. . . .

Achieving the Trance State

Entering the forbidden zones of the African-Haitian alternate reality necessitates some fundamental changes in the subatomic, atomic, and molecular composition of the adept. Passing from the ordinary state to the trance state involves great changes in energy level. Every particle begins to vibrate at a very high energy level. The four forces that maintain our structure in ordinary reality begin also to vibrate at a very high energy level, reaching velocity beyond that of light, other electromagnetic radiations, x-ray, strong force, w-force, and gravity, to attain that of tachyon or psychion state. A powerful magnetic field, a maelstrom of energy, is created inside and around the subject. In less singular cases, such as that of Uri Geller, very famous for his power of telekinesis, moving objects, and bending forks at a distance, the Stanford researchers defined him as one big walking magnetic field (Wilson 1172–1175). . . .

The high-energy state or the high-vibratory state induced by the trance throws the subject into that supergravitational dimension that can violate the conservation laws and attracts him into a black hole-like situation where singularities dominate. In that dimension the probabilities shift toward the energy part of the equation or wave-function reality with all its avatars . . . that state in which the ordinary laws of reality cease to apply, opening the door to other dimensions where the equivalence of mass and energy reigns. . . .

The abduction into that . . . other universe creates denizens of an intermediate nature between us and the shadow-matter world. The symbiotic alliance may give rise to creatures like baka, zombi, elves, fairies, and manikins. They come in different sizes and shapes and seem to crave nostalgically of the existence in our ordinary reality, but they have their boundary constraints and can manifest themselves into our world only for a short period. Some of them do not like our modern technological environment; most prefer the rustic and idyllic countryside. They prefer peasantry to city dwellers. It is possible that our electronic wizardry interferes with the wizardry of some species in that alternate reality. Some of them appear as permanent hybrids between animals and axionic entities; or between animal, human being, and vodouns; or human beings, plants, and vodouns; or simply human beings and loa. We have to remember that many of the loa like to be married to humans. In Haiti, the contract of marriage is produced in the format of an ordinary matrimony. What appears as an imitation of a three-dimensional event may have profound actualization in the world of naked singularities. That can give rise to creatures similar to the Nephilim of Genesis.

We do not know all the laws or principles governing the axionic, singular world of vodouns and similar entities, like we do not yet know all the laws of our ordinary reality. In the twentieth century, we have made great strides with quantum mechanics and its implications. Still many more secrets of nature remain to be discovered. There exists great complexity in either universe.

Note

1. Immaterial does not mean nonphysical. Energy as well as shadow matter is physical. Quantum physics deals with mass and wave functions that are physical.

References

March, Robert H. "Mind-Boggling Mysteries of Matter," *Science Year 1978*, pp. 182–95.

Métraux, Alfred. *Le Vaudou Haitien*. France: Gallimard, 1958.

Primack, Joel R. "The Case of the Dark Matter," *Science Year 1990*, pp. 114–27.

Turner, Michael S. "The University," *Science Year 1994*, pp. 174–99.

Wilson, Colin. "The Psychic Superstar," *Mysteries of Mind, Space and Time: The Unexplained*, volume 10 (Westport: H.S. Stuttman, 1992), pp. 1172–75.

Zombies Exist

Daniel Farson

Although popularized in countless Hollywood horror films like *Night of the Living Dead* and *28 Days Later*, actual accounts of real-life zombies are rare and treated with skepticism. Despite this, credible accounts of human beings evincing zombie-like behavior in Haiti have been given by respected American writers as early as the 1930s. In this excerpt from his book *Vampires, Zombies, and Monster Men*, author Daniel Farson finds that although many of these sightings relied heavily on verbal testimony and incomplete evidence, their consistency and the degree of dread with which most Haitians regard the possibility of becoming zombies suggest at least a kernel of truth behind such a bizarre, persistent myth. Nevertheless, Farson states that most zombies may simply be people who are mentally ill or under the influence of powerful drugs. Daniel Farson is also the author of *The Man Who Wrote Dracula: A Biography of Bram Stoker* and *Sacred Monsters*.

"The eyes were the worst. It was not my imagination. They were in truth like the eyes of a dead man, not blind, but staring, unfocused, unseeing. The whole face, for that matter, was bad enough. It was vacant, as if there was nothing behind it. It seemed not only expressionless, but incapable of expression. I had seen so much previously in Haiti that was outside ordinary normal experience that for the flash of a second I had a sickening, almost panicky lapse in which I thought, or rather felt, 'Great God, maybe this stuff is really true . . .'"

This was how William Seabrook described his encounter with one of the most horrifying creatures ever to step from the realms of the supernatural. For Seabrook was face-to-face with a zombie—a walking corpse. And in that moment he was prepared to believe all he had heard about zombies since he first arrived on the island of Haiti.

The zombie's fate is even worse than that of the vampire or the werewolf. The vampire returns to his loved ones. He may be recognized and lain to rest. The werewolf may be wounded and regain human form. But the zombie is a mindless automaton, doomed to live out a twilight existence of brutish toil. A zombie can move, eat, hear, even speak, but he has no memory of his past or knowledge of his present condition. He may pass by his own home or gaze into the eyes of his loved ones without a glimmer of recognition.

Neither ghost nor person, the zombie is said to be trapped, possibly forever, in that "misty zone that divides life from death." For while the vampire is the living dead, the zombie is merely the walking dead—a body without soul or mind raised from the grave and given a semblance of life through sorcery. He is the creature of the sorcerer, who uses him as a slave or hires him out—usually to work on the land.

Haiti is the home of the zombie, and the island abounds with stories of people who have died, been buried and reappeared as a walking corpse sometimes years later. One of the most famous cases, first recorded by American writer Zora Hurston in 1938, is still recounted in Haiti today. It concerns Marie, a lovely young society girl who died in 1909. Five years after her death, Marie was seen by some former school friends at the window of a house in Haiti's capital Port-au-Prince. The owner of the house refused to allow anyone to investigate, and Marie's father was reluctant to push the matter. Later, however, the house was searched, but by then the owner had disappeared and there was no trace of the girl. Meanwhile the news had spread all over Port-au-Prince, and to satisfy public opinion Marie's grave was opened. Inside was a skeleton too long for the coffin. Neatly folded alongside the skeleton were the clothes in which Marie had been buried.

People say that Marie had been dug up and used as a zombie until the sorcerer who had held her captive died, and his widow turned her over to a Catholic priest. After her schoolmates had seen her, it was said that her family smuggled her out of Haiti, dressed as a nun, and sent her to a convent in France. There she was later visited by her brother.

It is a sad aspect of most zombie stories, however, that no one generally comes to zombies' aid. Family and friends may never learn of the zombie's plight, or if they do, they are much too frightened to intervene. One mother told Zora Hurston about her son who had died and been buried. After the funeral friends stayed overnight with the grieving woman and her daughter. During the night the boy's sister awoke to the sound of chanting and of blows in the street outside. Then she clearly heard her brother's voice. Her screams awoke the rest of the house, and everyone looked out of the windows. Outside a grim procession was wending its way along the street, and in its midst was the boy they had buried that very day. As he stumbled sightlessly by, they all heard his anguished cry. "But such is the terror inspired by these ghouls," wrote Zora Hurston, "that no one, not even the mother or sister, dared to go out and attempt a rescue." The procession shuffled out of sight. The boy's sister subsequently went insane. . . .

The Basics of Voodoo

Voodoo is a formalized religion with its own gods and forms of worship. But it also has its sinister side—the voodoo of black magic, sorcery, and superstition, of monsters, murder, and raising the dead. Blood is an essential part of some ceremonies, usually involving the sacrifice of such animals as pigs, hens, and cockerels.

Voodoo ceremonies take place in *tonnelles*. These may be either simple rough huts with mud floors or an elaborate building, but they always contain a covered area for ritual dance. It is during the dance that worshipers undergo the central experience of voodoo worship—possession by the gods. The dancing, chanting, and throbbing of drums are said to generate an atmosphere in which god and worshiper may become one, and at the height of the dance the worshipers enter a state of trance—a sort of collective delirium—which ends in collapse.

A dancer may be possessed by any one of a huge number of gods and spirits, many of whom are still known by their African names. During possession the dancer is believed to *become* the god or spirit, adopting not only the god's personality but his or her physical appearance, gestures, and behavior. Thus a dancer possessed by the ancient spirit Papa Legba—guardian of the gateway to the other world and god of crossroads, whose symbol is a crutch—becomes apparently old and lame. Others, recognizing the spirit, run forward with sticks and crutches to help him. A sea god will row with invisible oars. A flirtatious female god will make a possessed man or woman assume mincing flaunting gestures. A traditional goddess from Dahomey called *Agassa*— a royal union of panther and woman—continues to exert her power in Haiti, causing possessed dancers to stiffen their fingers into claws. Evil spirits might throw a dancer into convulsions. Possession can last for several hours and be so absolute that the possessed walk on burning coals or hold their hands in boiling water without flinching, just as the members of some African tribes used to cut off their own fingers in a state of trance.

A British visitor to Haiti, Patrick Leigh Fermor, gives this interpretation of how possession—or the supposed incarnation of the gods in their worshipers—takes place. In his book *The Traveller's Tree*, written in 1950, he notes, "Every Haitian . . . from his earliest childhood, is spiritually geared for the event of incarnation; and he knows that the moment of miracle occurs in the dark *tonnelle* where the air is afloat with mysteries, and where the drums are already violently reacting on his nerves and brain . . . and so, when he has been brought by the drums, the dance, and the divine presence to a state of hysteria and physical collapse, a dormant self-hypnosis, finding no opposition, leaps to the surface of his brain and takes control."

Certainly it has been established by electrical recordings of the human brain that it is particularly sensitive to rhythmic stimulation. The *hungan*, or voodoo priest, may therefore increase suggestibility by altering the pitch and pace of the ceremonial rhythms. Hungans are also known to use magical powders and herbs as aids to possession, and it is said that even a substance as ordinary as pepper may be enough to bring on possession in the feverish atmosphere of a voodoo ceremony.

Whatever the trigger that induces possession, voodoo worshipers believe that the god cannot take over their body unless their soul is first displaced. The soul is believed to consist of two spirits: the *gros-bon-ange* (big good angel) and the *ti-bon-ange* (little good angel). The ti-bon-ange is what we might call a person's conscience. The gros-bon-ange is his essential soul—everything that makes him what he is.

Without the gros-bon-ange, the ti-bon-ange and the body lose contact. It is the gros-bon-ange that is displaced during possession, so that a person is no longer himself but the god who has taken over his body. Normally possession ends spontaneously, and the worshiper's gros-bon-ange is automatically restored to him. But sometimes the return to oneself will only happen with the hungan's help. Great care is also taken after a person's death to provide his disembodied soul with an alternative dwelling place. The soul, which first spends some time at the bottom of a river, is recalled by the hungan during a special ceremony, and placed in a sacred jar—a substitute for the physical body. It then becomes an ancestral spirit who will advise and protect his family. . . .

The voodoo sorcerer, or *bokor*, is a terrifying character who communes with the dead and practices all the darkest arts on behalf of himself and his clients. Sometimes hungan and sorcerer are one and the same person, for it is said that a priest must be well acquainted with the techniques of sorcery if he is to combat them successfully. A hungan might fight a curse with white magic one day, and cast a spell with black magic the next. Hungans can invoke good spirits, or evil ones like the *Zandor* who turn people into snakes or vampire bats. Voodooists maintain, however, that the true hungan will have nothing to do with sorcery, and there certainly are bokor who are not voodoo priests. The bokor inspire criminal societies, worship the devil, and gather in cemeteries to practice the sinister cult of the dead.

Such sorcerers make powders out of cemetery earth and dead men's bones to "send the dead" against an enemy. Spreading the powder outside the victim's door or across some path he often takes is enough to paralyze or kill him, unless another hungan works some counter-magic in time. Another dreaded custom is the dressing of a corpse in the clothes of an intended victim and concealing it in some secret place to rot away while the living person goes mad searching for it. As students of Haitian belief have pointed out, if the victim knows what is happening and believes in the force of the magic, it can easily have fatal results.

Haitians tell spine-chilling tales of corpses being dragged from the grave to serve the cruel will of the sorcerer. In his book *The Magic Island*, written in 1936, William Seabrook records this story of a young wife, Camille, and her husband Matthieu Toussel. On their first wedding anniversary Toussel took his wife to a feast soon after midnight. He insisted that Camille wear her bridal dress and she, being afraid of him, obeyed. As the couple entered a candlelit room laid for a banquet, Camille saw that there were four other guests, all in evening clothes. But none of them turned to greet her. Toussel excused their behavior, promising that after dinner all four men would drink and dance with her. His voice was odd and strained. Camille could see the fingers of one guest clutched, motionless, around a tilted, spilling wineglass. Seizing a candle she looked into his face—and realized she was sharing a banquet with four propped-up corpses.

The panic-stricken girl ran for her life, but she never recovered from her nightmare experience. Friends who returned to the scene later the same day found everything laid out exactly as she had described—but no trace of the silent guests nor of Toussel, who is said to have fled the island.

Legend or fact? The machinations of a sorcerer husband or the imaginings of an unbalanced wife? The Haitians who told Seabrook this story believed it was true. They knew other stories like it. Haitian children are raised on tales of black magic, bogies, and sorcerers' spells. Their mothers warn them never to play with their shadows, and tell them that the bokor or the *tonton macoute*—traveling voodoo magician—will get them if they don't behave—a threat that could have proved only too true under Haiti's dictator Dr. Francois Duvalier, whose strong private army was dubbed the *tontons macoute*.

It is this atmosphere of fear and superstition that has bred belief in the zombie. From cemetery cults and disinterred bodies it is but a short step to the idea of a corpse brought back to half-life by black magic—and some would say this was Toussel's intention for his dinner guests. Of all the supernatural horrors that sorcery may reserve for the unwary, becoming a zombie is the most dreaded fate of all, and a threat that even the most sophisticated may find hard to shrug off. Alfred Metraux, author of *Voodoo in Haiti*, made a study of zombies in the late 1950s. He says, "At Port-au-Prince there are few, even among the educated, who do not give some credence to these macabre stories."

One of the macabre stories that Metraux recorded concerns a young girl who rejected the advances of a powerful hungan. He stalked off, muttering threats about her future. Sure enough, the girl grew ill and died. For some reason, she was buried in a coffin too short for her, and her neck had to be bent to fit her in. While this was going on, a candle near the coffin was overturned, burning the girl's foot. Years later, people claimed to have seen the girl, apparently alive and clearly recognizable by her stoop and the burn on her foot. It was said that the jealous hungan had made her into a zombie, and kept her as a servant in his house until so much attention was drawn to the case that he was obliged to set her free.

This hungan was motivated by revenge—a common reason for the creation of zombies. Other times, zombies are made simply to provide cheap and uncomplaining labor when any suitable corpse will do. More rarely, they are the carefully chosen victims of a pact with the forces of evil, who demand payment in human souls for services rendered. For while Christians talk of selling one's soul to the devil, a voodoo follower sells the souls of others. In return for power, wealth, or some other favor, he must pledge the souls of those nearest and dearest to him. Each year the horrible sacrifice must be repeated until there are no more relatives or beloved friends left to give, and the person must then give himself. He too surrenders his soul. Then his body, like theirs, becomes a zombie.

Dark Rituals

Such pacts are made with the help of the bokor, and only he can create zombies. After dark he saddles a horse and rides, backward, to the victim's house. Placing his lips against a slit in the door he sucks out the person's soul, and traps it in a corked bottle. Shortly afterward the victim falls ill and dies. At midnight on the day of burial, the bokor goes with his assistants to the grave, opens it, and calls the victim's name. Because the bokor holds his soul, the dead person has to lift his head in answer. As he does so, the bokor passes the bottle containing the soul under the corpse's nose for a single brief instant. The dead person is then reanimated. Dragging him from the tomb, the bokor chains his wrists and beats him about the head to revive him further. Then he carefully closes the tomb, so no one will notice it has been disturbed.

Led by the bokor and his associates, the victim is first taken past his own house. This is said to insure that he will never again recognize his home and try to return there. He is then taken to the bokor's house or a voodoo temple, and given a secret drug. Some say this is an extract of poisonous plants like datura (jimson weed) or belladonna (deadly nightshade), which were sometimes used by the slaves of colonial days to kill their masters. Others maintain that the potion is made of drops that fall from a corpse's nose.

There are other methods of ensnaring a person's soul. A jar containing herbs and magical objects may be placed beneath a dying man's pillow to draw off the soul, or the soul of an insect or small animal may be substituted for the human soul. In neither case does the victim realize what is happening. It is even possible to take the soul from a person already dead. Whatever the method used, the soul plays the same part in the ritual at the tomb, and after the giving of the magic drug, all is complete. The victim has become a zombie—a hideous, mesmerized, walking corpse, ready to do the sorcerer's will.

Elaborate precautions are taken to prevent the sorcerer from raising the dead and creating a zombie. A family that can afford it may bury its dead beneath solid masonry. Others will make sure that the grave is dug in their own back yard or close to a busy road with plenty of passers-by. Since only a fresh or well-preserved corpse will serve the bokor's purpose, relatives may keep a continuous watch at the tomb until the body has decomposed. Sometimes the corpse is killed again, being shot through the head, injected with poison, or strangled. Occasionally it is buried with a dagger in its hand to defend itself. Often the body is placed face downward in the grave with its mouth full of earth, or its lips are sewn together so that it cannot speak to answer when the sorcerer calls its name.

Once people become zombies they can never escape from their deathly trance unless they taste salt (frequently a symbol of white magic). They then become aware of their fate and, knowing they are dead, will return to the grave forever.

In his book *The Invisibles*, British anthropologist Francis Huxley tells a story he heard from a Catholic priest of a zombie who wandered back to his own village in 1959. He was taken to the police station, but the police were too frightened to do anything and simply left him outside in the street. After several hours someone plucked up the courage to give the zombie a drink of salt water, and he then stammered his name. Later his aunt, who lived nearby, identified him. According to her, he had died and been buried four years before.

A priest was called and, after he arrived, the zombie revealed the name of the sorcerer for whom he and a band of other zombies had been forced to labor. The police, thoroughly scared now, sent a message to the sorcerer offering him his zombie back. However, two days later the zombie was found, well and truly dead this time—presumably killed by the sorcerer because of his damaging revelations. The sorcerer was eventually arrested, but his wife and the other zombies were never traced. . . .

Zora Hurston notes that such creatures were occasionally brought to a missionary by a bokor who had been converted—or by a sorcerer's widow who wished to be rid of them. She herself was one of the few visitors to Haiti to see, touch, and actually photograph a zombie. The zombie was Felicia Felix-Mentor, who had died of a sudden illness in 1907. In 1936 she was found wandering naked on the road near her brother's farm. Both her brother and her husband identified her as the woman they had buried 29 years before. She was in such a wretched condition that she was taken to the hospital, and it was there, a few weeks later, that Zora Hurston saw her. "The sight was dreadful," she wrote later. "That blank face with the dead eyes. The eyelids were white all around the eyes as if they had been burned with acid. There was nothing that you could say to her or get from her except by looking at her, and the sight of this wreckage was too much to endure for long."

So zombies or zombielike creatures do exist. But are they really walking corpses? Is it possible for a dead body to be given the semblance of life? Montague Summers, an authority on witchcraft and black magic, once wrote: "That necromancy can seemingly endow a dead body with life, speech, and action is not to be disputed, but the spell is invariably of short continuance and the operation, from the confession of sorcerers, is considered to be one of the most difficult and most dangerous in all witchcraft, a feat only to be accomplished by wizards who are foulest and deepest in infernal crime."

A spell of "short continuance" would hardly explain the reappearance after 29 years of Felicia Felix-Mentor. A far more likely explanation is that so-called zombies have never been dead at all. Some people have suggested that zombies are simply the doubles of persons who have died. If so, why do such doubles always have the characteristic zombie appearance and gait? Zombies are known for their expressionless and often downcast eyes, their blank faces, and shambling walk. They appear not to hear when spoken to, and their own speech, uttered in a nasal twang, is almost always incoherent. Often it consists only of grunts or guttural noises deep in the throat.

These are often the hallmarks of the mentally defective, and it seems probable that many alleged zombies are in fact morons concealed by their family and deliberately made out to be dead until they are seen again, perhaps many years later. Alfred Metraux was introduced to a zombie only to find a "wretched lunatic." On the next day this zombie was identified as a mentally deficient girl who had escaped from her home, where her parents normally kept her locked up.

Students of Haiti have pointed out that the harsh treatment meted out to zombies is no worse than the treatment of the mentally sick, who are commonly beaten to cow them into compliance. Once he had recovered from his initial shock at the sight of those "staring, unfocused, unseeing eyes," William Seabrook too concluded that the zombies he had seen were "nothing but poor ordinary demented human beings, idiots, forced to toil in the fields," rather than half-alive corpses.

What, then, of the reliable witnesses who have testified to the burial of some so-called zombies? Were they lying? Not all zombies started out as morons. What about the person friends remember as a sane, intelligent individual, who suddenly reappears as a vacant, gibbering wreck of his former self? This has to be a different kind of case.

Drugged and Buried

The answer comes from a surprising source—Article 246 of the old Haitian Criminal Code. "Also to be termed intention to kill," it states, "is the use of substances whereby a person is not killed but reduced to a state of lethargy, more or less prolonged, and this without regard to the manner in which the substances were used or what was their later result. If following the state of lethargy the person is buried, then the attempt will be termed murder."

From this it can be inferred that a zombie may really be a person buried and mourned by his family, and dragged from the grave by the bokor as the legend says. But he has been buried alive after being drugged into a deathlike trance from which he may never recover.

A prominent Haitian doctor interviewed by William Seabrook was convinced that at least some reported zombies were victims of this kind of treatment. Doctors with whom Zora Hurston discussed the case of Felicia Felix-

Mentor agreed. "We discussed at length the theories of how zombies come to be," she writes. "It was concluded that it is not a case of awakening the dead, but a semblance of death induced by some drug—some secret probably brought from Africa and handed down from generation to generation. . . . It is evident that it destroys that part of the brain which governs speech and will power. The victims can move and act but cannot formulate thought. The two doctors expressed their desire to gain this secret, but they realized the impossibility of doing so. These secret societies are secret. They will die before they will tell."

The idea, if not the making, of the zombie almost certainly originated in Africa, where legendary tales are still told of sorcerers who can raise the dead. The true zombie, however, is unique to Haiti. While cynics would say that so-called zombies must be lunatics or people temporarily in a state of trance, there are undoubtedly cases that can only be explained on a deeper and more sinister level. Today voodoo is often exploited as a tourist attraction, and spectacular displays of black magic may be mounted for the entertainment of foreigners and natives alike. Francis Huxley tells, for instance, of a magistrate who saw a hungan take a body from the grave and apparently reanimate it. Inside the grave the magistrate found a tube leading out to the air. The "corpse" was really the hungan's accomplice, and had been able to breathe in comfort while awaiting his resurrection.

Haitians know about hoaxes like this. Yet many of them still believe in zombies, and have a deep-rooted fear of joining their ranks. For while zombies may not be raised from the grave, they may well be people reduced by drugs to a state that is scarcely distinguishable from death. Who would say which fate is the worse? In either case, the zombie is truly one of the walking dead.

Zombies Are Created with the Use of Drugs

Wade Davis

Wade Davis is an ethnobotanist (a person who studies how people of a certain culture and region make use of indigenous plants) and was the host and cowriter of *Earthguide*, a series that aired on the Discovery channel. In 1985, he achieved literary and financial success with his autobiographical account of his investigations into the physiological and social aspects of Haitian zombification, *The Serpent and the Rainbow*, a book that served as the inspiration for a 1988 horror film of the same title. In it, Davis describes his infiltration of the Haitian secret societies known as the *Bizango*, whose practitioners manufactured a drug using tetrodotoxin, a poison extracted from female puffer fish. This drug, when injected into a human victim, was reputed to temporarily induce a physiological state simulating death, in effect creating "zombies," though by chemical rather than supernatural means. A subsequent volume, *Pas-*

sage of Darkness, offers more details on what ingredients such a drug would contain and whether it could actually exist. In the following excerpt from that volume, Davis concludes that not only is zombie powder real, but zombies produced by the drug continue to exist in Haiti, forced to serve as cheap slave labor for these *Bizango* societies as an unusually cruel form of social sanction. Davis's other books include *Nomads of the Dawn* and *Shadows in the Sun*.

The Zombie Project began in the spring of 1982 when the Botanical Museum at Harvard was contacted by the late Nathan S. Kline, eminent psychopharmacologist and then director of the Rockland State Research Institute of New York. Kline had worked in Haiti for more than thirty years; he knew [former Haitian president] François Duvalier and had been instrumental in establishing the country's first and only modern psychiatric facility, the Centre de Psychiatrie et Neurologie Mars-Kline. The center's first director was Lamarque Douyon, a Haitian psychiatrist who had trained at McGill University, where his work had come to the attention of Heinz Lehmann, another psychopharmacologist and a close colleague of Nathan Kline's. Since assuming the directorship of the psychiatric institute in 1961, Douyon, in collaboration with both Kline and Lehmann, had been systematically investigating all popular reports of the appearance of zombies, the infamous living dead of Vodoun folklore. In 1980 their efforts were rewarded by the discovery of the extraordinary case of Clairvius Narcisse.

What made this case noteworthy was the fact that Narcisse had been pronounced dead in 1962 at the Albert Schweitzer Hospital, an American-directed philanthropic institution that maintains precise and accurate records.

Therefore, in addition to the death certificate, Douyon was able to obtain a medical dossier outlining the history of the case and the particular symptoms suffered by the patient at the time of his demise. According to these records, Narcisse was pronounced dead on 2 May by two attending physicians—one an American, both American-trained—and his death and subsequent burial eight hours later were witnessed by family members. In 1980 a man claiming to be Narcisse returned to his village and introduced himself, by a boyhood nickname, to his sister. He stated that he had been made a zombie eighteen years before by his brother because of a land dispute.

The case was studied at length by Kline and Douyon. With the help of Narcisse's family, Douyon devised a series of questions concerning intimate aspects of the family past. These Narcisse answered correctly. Based on the results of this questionnaire, the testimony of villagers, family members, and physicians, forensic examination by Scotland Yard of the fingerprints on the death certificate, and the reasonable assumption that there was no social or economic incentive to perpetrate a fraud, Douyon and Kline concluded that the case was legitimate. In other words, they suggested that Clairvius Narcisse had been mistakenly diagnosed as dead, buried alive, and, having survived a period of time in the coffin, had been taken from the grave, presumably by the one who had perpetrated the deed.

A Folk Toxin?

If the case of Clairvius Narcisse was to be believed, there had to be a material explanation, and the attention of the medical team shifted to the possible existence of a folk toxin which had long been rumored to be involved in the process of zombification. It was, of course, theoretically possible that a folk preparation might exist which, if administered in the proper dosage, would lower the metabolic state of the victim to such a level that he or she would be considered dead. In fact, however, the recipient of the toxin would remain alive, and an antidote, properly administered, could then restore him or her at the appropriate time. The medical potential of such a drug, particularly in the field of anesthesia, could be significant, but no one had yet obtained its formula. Douyon sent one sample of the reputed powder to Kline's laboratory in New York, but it proved to be chemically inert. Moreover, Douyon was unable to observe the preparation of the powder, nor did he have an opportunity to collect voucher specimens of the crude ingredients. He reported merely that a toxic powder and its antidote existed by folk record, that the poison was placed on the ground in the form of a cross, and that the potential victim had merely to walk across it to succumb.

Nathan Kline, despite his high-level contacts and his thirty years' experience in the country, also failed in his attempts to identify the elusive toxin. Indeed, though the preparation of the poison is specifically referred to in the Haitian penal code and reports of its existence by both popular and ethnographic literature date back well into the nineteenth century, no researcher had managed to discover its ingredients. It was with this precise assignment of obtaining samples of the folk toxin—if in fact it existed—and documenting its preparation that I was asked to join the Zombie Project. . . . In the end, the identity of the folk toxin was established, but perhaps more significantly, the interdisciplinary approach that led to its discovery and a glimpse at the process of zombification also suggested cultural aspects of great importance. Evidence suggests that zombification is a form of social sanction imposed by recognized corporate bodies—the poorly known and clandestine secret Bizango societies—as one means of maintaining order and control in local communities.

Any presentation of results, of course, reflects a logical progression of ideas that, to say the least, was not at all evident at the beginning of the project. When I was first asked to go to Haiti, my own notion of zombies, if indeed I had one, was infected with misconceptions derived from a slew of sensational films and pulp fiction. As I began the investigation it became clear that these misconceptions would not be contradicted or clarified by the ethnographic literature. Anthropologists on the whole had perfunctorily dismissed the phenomenon as superstition. Reported cases that had at least the veneer of legitimacy, and which collectively demanded explanation, were ignored. Although it was mentioned in many major ethnographic and popular publications, the folk toxin had never been systematically investigated. The entire notion of zombies was seen as little more than a symptom of the Haitian peasant's notorious instincts for the phantasmagoric. Indeed, for a phenomenon that had so electrified the rest of the world, and which had been used in an explicitly racist way to denigrate both a people and their religion, there was a glaring absence of serious academic research that might prove once and for all whether zombies of any form were to be found in Haiti.

Clearly the elusive poison was critical to both the Narcisse case and the zombie problem in general. Without it, one was obliged to consider the phenomenon as magical belief, the Narcisse case itself a fraud. Therefore, the initial phase of the project consisted of the formulation of a hypothesis by a careful consideration of the ethnopharmacological literature and the field testing of that hypothesis in Haiti. From preliminary reports, it appeared that the preparation had to be topically active, capable of inducing a prolonged psychotic state, and that the initial dosage had to bring on a deathlike stupor. The substance had to be extremely potent and, because both the toxin and its purported antidote were likely to be organically derived, their source had to be a plant or animal currently found in Haiti.

The Search for Zombie Powder

An obvious candidate was *Datura stramonium* L., a psychoactive plant known to induce stupor in high dosages, and which in Haitian Creole has the provocative name *concombre zombi*—the zombie's cucumber. The plant owes its activity to a series of tropane alkaloids and, interestingly, the recognized medical antidote for these compounds is derived from a West African liana, *Physostigma venenosum* Balf.—a plant employed in ritual context as an ordeal poison by precisely the indigenous groups that were sold into bondage to Saint Domingue.

During the spring and summer of 1982 I tested this hypothesis in the field in Haiti. It proved to be false. Neither in the modest national herbarium nor in extensive field surveys was any evidence found to suggest that *P. venenosum* had been naturalized in Haiti. Feral populations of the weedy *D. stramonium* were common, particularly in old fields, but no evidence suggested that the plant was an ingredient in the zombie preparations. Nevertheless, this initial period achieved several important research goals. Working first with Douyon and subsequently alone, I conducted extensive interviews with Clairvius Narcisse, his family, and a number of villagers, as well as with the family of Francina Illeus, a second reputed zombie who remained at the time in a catatonic state. These interviews added considerably to the body of information on Narcisse and Illeus and allowed me to introduce the cases into the technical ethnopharmacological literature (Davis 1983).

Next, with the assistance of a prominent Port-au-Prince houngan, I was able to establish within a very short time extensive contacts with numerous sorcerers (*bokor*) and Vodoun priests (*houngan*). In April 1982, working through these contacts, I met an individual who was reputedly capable of preparing the zombie powder. After a complicated series of negotiations, I was able to purchase a sample of the powder and its "antidote" and observe their preparation, at the same time obtaining complete sets of voucher specimens of all the raw ingredients. Following this initial success, I attempted to obtain the preparation at other localities throughout Haiti. Between April and November 1982, I studied five other preparations in the communities of Saint Marc, Gonaïves, Léogane, and Petite Rivière de Nippes. Oral interviews at two other communities, Montrouis and Archaie, verified the critical ingredients. This fieldwork, together with subsequent collections made in the spring of 1984, produced a total of eight preparations—a significant number by ethnobiological standards.

Although I have detailed elsewhere the complete process of obtaining these preparations and the voucher specimens (Davis 1985), there are several important points to note here. First, the preparation of the zombie powder is not the "dark secret" that most of the literature has assumed it to be. . . . The Vodounist believes emically that the preparation is only a support of the magical force of the sorcerer, and it is this power, not a poison, that creates the zombie. However, like all the elements of the sorcerer's repertoire, the formula of the zombie powder is highly valued and obtaining it necessitated a complex process of negotiation. To be sure, it cost money, and there is an odd and unwarranted sense among some ethnographic fieldworkers that data obtained by financial remuneration is somehow tainted. This is, in general, an arrogant proposition, as it assumes that the informant has nothing better to do than provide free information to a foreign investigator. In Haiti, such an attitude is not only unjust but counterproductive, for within the Vodoun society to do something for nothing is generally seen as "less a manifestation of generosity than as a sign of gullibility, is less a virtue than a weakness (Murray 1977, 596). The Haitians themselves pay the bokor for his knowledge and powders, and so should the ethnobiologist.

This does not mean that money should be thrown at a problem, or that financial payment alone would have obtained the correct formula of the zombie powder. Those who have abrasively attempted to buy, bribe, or threaten the bokor in the past have been unsuccessful. Indeed, in the process of successfully obtaining any ethnographic information, there is an ineffable quality to the interaction between researcher and informant, impossible to quantify but often critical to the legitimacy of the data and the overall value of the research. This quality is reflected in gesture, attitude, spontaneous repartee, and other moments that seldom find their way into print but whose importance is appreciated by all fieldworkers. Establishing a positive relationship with an entire network of houngan and bokor was the critical hidden element in the Zombie Project, and the character of that relationship, its positive and negative aspects, accounts directly for any successes or shortcomings in this study.

The Necessary Ingredient

The second major phase of the Zombie Project began in the fall of 1982 upon my return to the Botanical Museum. Taxonomic identification of all the ingredients in the reputed poisons and antidotes, along with additional readings in the literature, revealed that:

1. The ingredients and composition of the various antidotes are completely inconsistent from one region to the next, and the constituents themselves are probably chemically inert or else are used in insufficient quantities to result

in any pharmacological activity.

2. The poisons contain a plethora of ingredients. In general, these ingredients fall into three broad categories. First, human remains—dried viscera, shavings of skulls, tibia, etc.—are included for magical reasons in every preparation. Second, plants and animals known to be pharmacologically active are added. Third, all the preparations contain elements that severely irritate the skin—ground glass, plants with urticating trichomes or toxic resins—and the inclusion of these irritants, several of which may induce self-inflicted wounds, is related to the way the preparation is applied. The powders are administered topically to open wounds or abraded skin and may be applied more than once.

3. Among the various preparations, there is one consistent ingredient of great interest: various species of marine fish of the order Tetraodontiformes, which contain in their viscera tetrodotoxin, an extremely potent neurotoxin.

This discovery proved highly significant, for the effects of tetrodotoxin poisoning have been well documented, particularly in Japan where related toxic species have long been consumed as delicacies. With the assistance of the staff of the National Museum of Medicine in Washington, D.C., and with the active cooperation of Bruce Halstead, who helped me obtain translations of the early Japanese biomedical documents, I undertook an extensive review of the medical literature. By comparing the symptoms of tetrodotoxication as described in that literature with the constellation of symptoms recorded from the zombies, it became clear that tetrodotoxin offered a material basis for the zombie phenomenon. In brief, the toxin induces a state of complete peripheral paralysis, marked by imperceptibly low metabolic levels and the retention of consciousness on the part of the patient up until the moment of death. Correlation, for the first time, of this obscure literature with the

case histories from Haiti suggested that the folk preparation, if administered in the proper dosage, could in fact
bring on a state of apparent death that might allow an individual to be misdiagnosed and buried alive. Indeed, the
literature reported instances in Japan and the South Pacific,
completely unrelated to zombification, in which poison
victims had in fact been mistaken for dead and placed in
their coffins ready for burial.

Following the identification of the raw ingredients of the
poison, the powder itself was tested on laboratory animals
by Leon Roizin at Columbia Presbyterian Hospital in New
York. A topical application of the powder to the abdominal
surfaces of white rats produced shallow, faint breathing and
decreased spontaneous activity. Within thirty minutes the
rats lay immobilized; for three to six hours they displayed
only mild response to corneal stimulation, pain, and sound
and showed evidence of hypothermia. From six to nine
hours after administration of the powder, they appeared comatose and showed no response at all to external stimuli.
The electroencephalograph (EEG) continued to monitor
central nervous system activity, and the hearts were not affected. Certain rats remained immobilized for twenty-four
hours and then recovered with no apparent sign of injury.
In a separate experiment, the powder was applied topically
to the shaved belly of a rhesus monkey. After twenty minutes the monkey's usual aggressive behavior diminished
and it retired to a corner of its cage and assumed a catatonic
posture. The animal remained immobilized for nine hours.
Recovery was complete (Leon Roizin, pers. comm., 1982).

These preliminary laboratory results, together with discoveries in the field and the biomedical literature, suggested
strongly that there could be an ethnopharmacological basis
to the zombie phenomenon. The consistent and critical ingredients in the poison appeared to be marine fish contain-

ing known toxins capable of inducing a physical state that could allow an individual to be misdiagnosed as dead. That Narcisse's symptoms are consistent with the known effects of tetrodotoxin suggests the possibility that he was exposed to the poison. If this does not prove that he was a zombie, it does, at least, substantiate his account.

The formula of the poison provides a possible means by which an individual might, under rare circumstances, be made to appear dead, but the physical constituents alone explain very little about the zombie phenomenon. Any psychoactive drug possesses a completely ambivalent potential. It induces a certain condition, but that condition is only raw material, which is then worked upon by particular cultural and psychological forces and expectations. Until those expectations are understood, one cannot claim to know anything about the zombie phenomenon.

Why Make Zombies?

Therefore, the third phase of the Zombie Project focused exclusively on the emic interpretation of zombification and involved a complete immersion in the closed system of spiritual and magical belief that typifies the Vodoun worldview. After extensive work in the field with numerous bokor, it became clear to me that their conception of zombification bears little resemblance to what has been reported in the ethnographic literature. In brief, the Vodounist believes that anyone who dies an unnatural death—one caused by the intervention of sorcery—may be claimed as a zombie. It is not a poison but the performance of a magical rite by the bokor that creates a zombie; zombification is perceived as strictly a magical process totally dependent on the special and esoteric powers of the bokor. The bokor gains power by capturing the victim's *ti bon ange*—that component of the Vodoun soul that creates personality, character, and will-power. A zombie appears cataleptic precisely because it has no *ti bon ange*. Robbed of the soul, the body is but an empty vessel subject to the commands of an alien force, the one who maintains control of the *ti bon ange*. It is the notion of external forces taking control of the individual that is so terrifying to the Vodounist. In splitting the sacred components of man, the bokor makes two kinds of zombies: the *zombi éfface* or *zombi astral*, which is a spirit; and the *zombi corps cadavre*, which is the zombie of the flesh. To the Vodounist both forms of zombification are equally real, but for the latter to exist one must discover an etic, or in this case pharmacological, cause. The application of the toxic preparation is, for the bokor, only one means of causing the prerequisite unnatural death. . . .

Yet, while the potency of the sorcerer's spell and the powder itself suggest a means by which both physical and spiritual zombies may be created, they nevertheless explain very little about the process of zombification within the context of Haitian traditional society. The peasant knows that the fate of the zombie is enslavement. Yet given the availability of cheap labor and the debilitated physical condition of the zombies, there is obviously no economic incentive to create a workforce of indentured labor. Instead, the concept of slavery implies that the victim of zombification suffers a fate worse than death—the loss of individual freedom implied by enslavement, and the sacrifice of individual identity and autonomy implied by the loss of the *ti bon ange*. It must be emphasized that the fear in Haiti is not *of* zombies, but rather of *becoming* a zombie. This fear is pervasive and has given rise to a complex body of folklore that continues to influence behavior. Both the threat and the fact of zombification confer on the bokor a potent means of social control if he chooses to use it. Under what circumstances, then, does the bokor invoke this power? Or, to rephrase the question, why is someone chosen to become a victim in the first place? These questions prompted the final and no doubt the most significant phase of the research project.

From extensive examination of the cases of Narcisse and other reputed zombies, it did not appear that the threat of zombification was invoked in either a criminal or a random way. Significantly, all of the reputed zombies were pariahs within their communities at the time of their demise. Moreover, the bokor who administer the spells and powders commonly live in the communities where the zombies are created; regardless of personal power, it is unlikely that a bokor who was not supported by the community could continue to create zombies for long, and for his own personal gain, with impunity. A more plausible view is that zombification is a social sanction administered by the bokor in complicity with, and in the services of, the members of his community. In fact, the authority to create a zombie may rest not solely with an individual bokor but with the secret society of which he is a member.

The last phase of the Zombie Project addressed the possible connection between the Bizango secret societies and zombification. With the assistance of established contacts, I was able to work directly among several Bizango societies for a four-month period in the spring and summer of 1984. The results of that effort . . . represent perhaps the only first-hand account of the structure and function of these clandestine societies ever to enter the ethnographic literature. In short, these contemporary secret societies constitute a force, if not an institution, parallel to the Vodoun temples headed by the houngan. They are polycephalous; each local hierarchical organization is headed by an *emperor*, who is attended by one or more *presidents* and *queens.* Members recognize each other by means of ritualized greetings learned at initiation, and by identification papers known as passports. The societies have their own drumbeats and body of songs and dances, and they are active by night. Like the secret societies of West Africa from which they are descended, the Bizango societies appear to be an important arbiter of social life among the peasantry. They constitute a force that protects community resources, particularly land, as they define the power boundaries of the village. Sorcery and poison are their traditional weapons, and there exists within the Bizango a complex judicial process by which those who violate the code of the society may be sanctioned. My research suggests that zombification represents the ultimate social sanction invoked by the societies. In addition, there is strong evidence . . . that the secret societies may be the key to understanding recent Haitian political history—in particular, the meteoric rise of the *Tonton Macoute* under François Duvalier. There can be no doubt that the Bizango societies were critical to the Duvalier regime or that their failure to support his son, Jean-Claude, was in no small part responsible for the sudden collapse of his government.

The ethnobiological search for the Haitian zombie powder unveiled ethnographic and historical vistas of considerable importance. In offering a general theory to account for zombification, this research has also highlighted the sorcerer's remarkable knowledge of natural products, identified what may be the first verified zombies, and clarified the emic/etic confusion that has plagued previous research on the subject. The network of secret societies, with their elaborate judicial function, their sanctions, and their utilization of folk toxins, may be traced in a direct lineage to the maroon bands of colonial Saint Domingue and even beyond to the secret societies of West Africa.

References

Davis, E.W. 1983. "The Ethnobiology of the Haitian Zombi." *Journal of Ethnopharmacology* 9 (1): 85–104.

———. 1985. *The Serpent and the Rainbow*. New York: Simon and Schuster.

Murray, G.F. 1977. "The Evolution of Haitian Peasant Land Tenure: A Case Study in Agrarian Adaptation to Population Growth." Ph.D. diss., Columbia University.

Chapter 2

Fact or Fiction?

The Power of
Voodoo Is
Not Real

Marie Laveau Was a Fraud

Joe Nickell

Marie Laveau is the quintessential figure associated with voodoo in the United States. During the mid-1800s she reigned as the "Voodoo Queen" of New Orleans, holding elaborate ceremonies and practicing fortune-telling. Much of her reputation, according to author Joe Nickell, is founded on nothing more than shrewd business acumen and a brilliance for showmanship. Marie's methods of giving the impression she was clairvoyant ranged from exploiting her position as a hairdresser for gossip collecting to blackmailing her enemies and competitors into silence. Joe Nickell is Senior Research Fellow of the Committee for the Scientific Investigation of Claims of the Paranormal and the author of *Real-Life X-Files*.

Voodoo in New Orleans can scarcely be separated from its dominant figure, Marie Laveau, about whom many legends

Joe Nickell, "Voodoo in New Orleans," *Skeptical Inquirer*, January/February 2002, pp. 15–18. Copyright © 2002 by Committee for the Scientific Investigation of Claims of the Paranormal. Reproduced by permission.

swirl. According to one source (Hauck 1996):

> She led voodoo dances in Congo Square and sold charms
> and potions from her home in the 1830s. Sixty years later
> she was still holding ceremonies and looked as young as she
> did when she started. Her rites at St. John's Bayou on the
> banks of Lake Pon[t]chartrain resembled a scene from hell,
> with bonfires, naked dancing, orgies, and animal sacrifices.
> She had a strange power over police and judges and suc-
> ceeded in saving several criminals from hanging.

Writer Charles Gandolfo (1992), author of *Marie Laveau
of New Orleans*, states: "Some believe that Marie had a mysterious birth, in the sense that she may have come from the
spirits or as an envoy from the Saints." On the other hand a
plaque on her supposed tomb, placed by the Catholic
Church, refers to her as "this notorious 'voodoo queen.'"

Who was the real Marie Laveau? She began life as the il-
legitimate daughter of a rich Creole plantation owner,
Charles Laveaux, and his Haitian slave mistress. Sources
conflict but Marie may have been born in New Orleans in
1794. In 1819 she wed Jacques Paris who, like her, was a
free person of color, but she was soon abandoned or wid-
owed. About 1826, she began a second, common-law marriage to Christophe de Glapion, another free person of
color, with whom she would have fifteen children.

Marie was introduced to voodoo by various "voodoo
doctors," practitioners of a popularized voodoo that emphasized curative and occult magic and seemed to have a
decidedly commercial aspect. Her own practice began when
she teamed up with a "heavily tattooed Voodoo doctor"—
known variously as Doctor John, Bayou John, John Bayou,
etc.—who was "the first commercial Voodooist in new Orleans to whip up potions and gris-gris for a price" (Gandolfo 1992, 11). Gris-gris or "juju" refers to magic charms or
spells, often conjuring bags containing such items as bones,
herbs, charms, snake skin, etc., tied up in a piece of cloth

(Antippas 1988, 16). Doctor John reportedly confessed to friends that his magic was mere humbuggery. "He had been known to laugh," writes Robert Tallant in *Voodoo in New Orleans* (1946, 39), "when he told of selling a gullible white woman a small jar of starch and water for five dollars."

In time Marie decided to seek her own fortune. Working as a hairdresser, which put her in contact with New Orleans' social elite, she soon developed a clientele to whom she dispensed potions, gris-gris bags, voodoo dolls, and other magical items. She now sought supremacy over her rivals, some fifteen "voodoo queens" in various neighborhoods. According to a biographer (Gandolfo 1992, 17):

> Marie began her take-over process by disposing of her rival queens. . . . If her rituals or gris-gris didn't work, Marie (who was a statuesque woman, to say the least) met them in the street and physically beat them. This war for supremacy lasted several years until, one by one, all of the former queens, under a pledge, agreed to be sub-queens. If they refused, she ran them out of town.

By age thirty-five Marie Laveau had become New Orleans' most powerful voodoo queen—then or since. She won the approval of the local priest by encouraging her followers to attend mass. While she charged the rich abundantly, she reportedly gave to the needy and administered to the suffering. Her most visible activities, however, were her public rituals. By municipal decree (from 1817) slaves were only permitted to dance publicly at a site called Congo Square. "These public displays of Voodoo ceremonies, however, revealed nothing of the real religion and became merely entertainment for the curious whites" (Antippas 1988, 14–15). More "secret" rituals—including fertility rituals—took place elsewhere, notably on the shore of Lake Pontchartrain.

It is difficult at this remove to assess just how much of Marie's rituals was authentic voodoo practice and how much was due to her "incredible imagination and an obsession for the extreme." She staged rituals that were "simulated orgies." Men and women danced in abandonment after drinking rum and seeming to become possessed by various *loas* [supernatural entities]. Seated on her throne, Marie directed the action when she was not actually participating. She kept a large snake called Le Grand Zombi that she would dance with in veneration of Damballah, shaking a gourd rattle to summon that snake deity and repeating over and over, "Damballah, ye-ye-ye!"

Once a year Marie presided over the ritual of St. John's Eve. It began at dusk on June 23 and ended at dawn on the next day, St. John's day. Hundreds attended, including reporters and curious onlookers, each of whom was charged a fee. Drum beating, bonfires, animal sacrifice, and other elements—including nude women dancing seductively—characterized the extended ritual. Offerings were made to the appropriate *loas* for protection, including safeguarding children and others from the Cajun bogeyman, Loup-Garou, a werewolf that supposedly fed on the blood of victims (Gandolfo 1992, 18–23).

Magic or Myth?

Claims regarding Marie Laveau's alleged powers persist. She represented herself as a seer and used fortune-telling techniques such as palmistry (Gandolfo 1992, 26). There is no evidence that Marie's clairvoyant abilities were any more successful than those of any other fortuneteller. We know that people attest to the accuracy of a reading because they do not understand the clever techniques involved, like "cold reading." So called because it is accomplished without any foreknowledge, this is an artful method of fishing for information from the sitter while convincing him or her that it comes from a mystical source (Hyman 1977).

Actually, many of Marie's readings may not have been so "cold" after all. Far from lacking prior information about her clients, she reputedly used her position as a hairdresser for gossip collecting, discovering "that her women clients would talk to her about anything and everything and would divulge some of their most personal secrets to her" (Gandolfo 1992, 12). She also reputedly "developed a chain of household informants in most of the prominent homes" (Antippas 1988, 16).

Doubtless such intelligence gathering would be helpful to a fortune-telling enterprise (just as "mediumistic espionage" was utilized by later spiritualists [Keene 1976, 27]). It could also be beneficial to a business of dispensing charms, like Marie's:

> Most of her work for the ladies involved love predicaments. Marie knew the personal secrets of judges, priests, lawyers, doctors, ship captains, architects, military officers, politicians, and most of New Orleans's other leading citizens. She used her knowledge of their indiscretions and blackmailed them into doing whatever she wanted. She was then financially reimbursed by her elite female clients. Most of the time, this was how her love potions and gris-gris worked, which is apparently 100% of the time (Gandolfo 1992, 12).

Such tactics may help explain the claim, mentioned earlier, that Marie "had a strange power over police and judges and succeeded in saving several criminals from hanging" (Hauck 1996). But we should beware of taking such claims too seriously. When we seek to learn the facts, we soon realize we have entered the realm of folklore. There are, for example, rather conflicting versions of one case, ca. 1830, in which an unidentified young man was charged with "a crime" (rape, according to one source) and at the request of his father Marie performed certain rituals. Supposedly the case was either dismissed or the young man acquitted, and Marie was rewarded with a cottage on Rue St. Ann. However, as one writer concedes, "No one is sure how Marie actually won the case. . . ." Therefore, of course, there is no evidence that she did (Gandolfo 1992, 14–15; cf. Tallant 1946, 58; Martinez 1956, 17–19).

Legends of Marie's beneficent aspect are rivaled by those of her sinister one. A story in this regard involves the alleged hex of a New Orleans businessman, J.B. Langrast, in the 1850s. Langrast supposedly provoked Marie's ire by publicly denouncing her and accusing her of everything from robbery to murder. Soon, gris-gris in the form of roosters' heads began to appear on his doorstep. As a consequence, Langrast reportedly grew increasingly upset and eventually fled New Orleans (Nardo and Belgum 1991, 89–92).

I have traced the Langrast story to a 1956 book of Mississippi folktales which describes the "businessman" as a junk dealer and bigamist (Martinez 1956, 78–83). Such a man might have various reasons for leaving town. Claims that Marie Laveau invoked a *loa* to curse Langrast with insanity are invalidated by a complete lack of proof that he ever became insane. In fact his alleged flight could easily be attributed to simple fear, the belief that "Marie Laveau's followers might kill him if he stayed" (Nardo and Belgum 1991, 90–91).

Marie II

Among the most fabulous legends about Marie Laveau is an often-repeated one alleging "her perpetual youth" (Hauck 1996). According to a segment of "America's Haunted Houses" (1998) which aired on the Discovery Channel, Marie was "said to be over 100 years old when she died and as beautiful as ever." Moreover, "There were some unexplained and mysterious sightings of the great Voodoo Queen even after her death," writes Gandolfo (1992, 29). "People would swear on a stack of bibles that they saw Marie Laveau herself." Indeed, he adds, "A number of people say they were at a ritual in the summer of 1919 given by the Great Queen."

The solution to this enigma is the fact that, according to Tallant (1946, 52), there were "at least two Marie Laveaus." The first Marie, the subject of our previous discussions, died June 15, 1881. Her obituaries say she was then ninety-eight ("Marie Lavaux" 1881; "Death" 1881). One of the same obituaries ("Death" 1881) states more credibly that she had been twenty-five when she wed, consistent with her having been born in 1794, as most sources now agree, and thus about eighty-seven when she died. Indeed, the doctor who attended Marie at the end publicly stated his doubts that she was as old as her family had claimed, and he judged her age to be in the late eighties (Tallant 1946, 117).

Whatever her actual age, far from appearing to be a figure of eternal youth, Marie Laveau spent her last years "old and shrunken," stripped of her memory, and lying in a back room of her cottage (Tallant 1946, 88, 115). In her stead was her daughter, Marie Laveau II. The younger Marie gradually took over her mother's business activities, which included running a house on Lake Pontchartrain where rich Creole men could have "appointments" with young mulatto girls (Tallant 1946, 65–66). She died in 1897.

The claim that Marie Laveau was active in 1919 is thought to have been based on a third Marie, possibly a granddaughter (Gandolfo 1992, 29), or another voodoo queen with whom she was confused.

In carrying on her mother's work, Marie II had business cards printed, billing her not as a voodooienne but as a "Healer." According to Tallant (1946, 93):

> The Laveau ways of performing homeopathic magic were endless. Sick people were often brought to the house to receive the benefit of a cure by Marie II. A person bitten by a snake was told to get another live snake of any sort, cut its

head off "while it was angry" and to tie this head to the wound. This was to be left attached until sunrise of the following day. Sometimes her practices contained an element of medical truth, embracing the use of roots and herbs that contained genuine curative elements. For sprains and swellings she used hot water containing Epsom salts and rubbed the injured parts with whiskey, chanting prayers and burning candles at the same time, of course. For other ailments she administered castor oil, to the accompaniment of incantations and prayer.

Like other occult healers, Marie obviously took advantage not only of the occasional "element of medical truth" but also other factors, including the body's own natural healing mechanisms and the powerful effects of suggestion.

References

"America's Haunted Houses." 1998. Discovery Channel. First aired May 24.

Antippas, A.P. 1988. *A Brief History of Voodoo: Slavery & the Survival of the African Gods.* New Orleans, Louisiana: Marie Laveau's House of Voodoo.

"Death of Marie Laveau." 1881. Obituary in *Daily Picayune,* n.d. (after June 15), clipping reproduced in Gandolfo 1992, 38; text quoted in full in Tallant 1946, 113–116.

Gandolfo, Charles. 1992. *Marie Laveau of New Orleans.* New Orleans, Louisiana: New Orleans Historic Voodoo Museum.

———. N.d. Museum guide sheet. New Orleans Historic Voodoo Museum.

Gould, Virginia. 1997. "Marie Laveau," in Darlene Clark Hine, ed. *Facts on File Encyclopedia of Black Women in America: The Early Years 1617–1899.* New York: Facts on File, 123–124.

Hauck, Dennis William. 1996. *Haunted Places: The National Directory.* New York: Penguin Books, 192, 193.

Hurbon, Laënnec. 1995. *Voodoo: Search for the Spirit.* New York: Harry N. Abrams.

Hyman, Ray. 1977. "Cold-reading: How to convince strangers that you know all about them." SKEPTICAL INQUIRER 1(2): 18–37.

Keene, M. Lamar, 1976. *The Psychic Mafia.* Reprinted Amherst, New York: Prometheus Books, 1997, 19–38.

"Marie Lavaux [*sic*]." 1881. Obituary in *New Orleans Democrat,* June 17, reproduced in Gandolfo 1992, 37.

Martinez, Raymond J. 1956. *Mysterious Marie Laveau, Voodoo Queen, and Folk Tales Along the Mississippi.* Reprinted New Orleans: Hope Publications, n.d.

Nardo, Don, and Erik Belgum. 1991. *Great Mysteries: Voodoo: Opposing Viewpoints.* San Diego, California: Greenhaven Press.

Tallant, Robert. 1946. *Voodoo in New Orleans.* Reprinted Gretna, Louisiana: Pelican Publishing Company, 1990.

Voodoo Is Real but Not Supernatural

Michael White

Michael White, the author of the following piece, argues that voodoo priests have the ability to create zombies and harm people with hexes. However, they do so not by using supernatural powers but through a combination of social conditioning and drugs. Terror at being "hexed" and the social ostracizing of the victim cause enough stress to induce cardiac arrest in a true believer in voodoo, making it seem as if the magic of the hex itself were responsible for the death. Similarly, zombies are produced by administering calculated amounts of physical punishment, drugs, and universal brainwashing techniques. White was formerly science editor of British *GQ* and director of scientific studies at d'Overbroeck's College in Oxford, England. He has written several books on scientific topics and was a consultant for the Discovery Channel's series *The Science of the Impossible*.

Those who practice Voodoo believe in a God, a deity they call *Djo* or *Mawu;* but this God differs fundamentally from the Christian God because they think that Djo or Mawu is far too important to interfere in earthly matters. Followers of Voodoo believe that when a human is born, they are mere animals but become infused with a spirit called the *loa,* placed inside you as a guide during an initiation ceremony. Another aspect of your being is the *ti bon ange,* or "little good angel," which is roughly equivalent to the "will." According to the Voodoo religion, at the initiation where the spirit imbues the body, the *ti bon ange* may be extracted and stored in a jar in the inner sanctum of the temple. When the owner of this life force dies, the jar is opened to allow their *ti bon ange* to hover over the dead person's grave for seven days. The purpose of leading a good life is to enrich the *ti bon ange* so that after sixteen incarnations a human may return to God. . . .

Putting aside the purely religious aspects of Voodoo and its comparisons with other faith systems, let us look at the controversial elements of its practice and claims for the creation of zombies, and the power to influence matter at a distance purely by the power of the mind. There are two fundamental and supposedly powerful "supernatural" angles to explore—the spirit world of the Haitian priests and their ability to raise the dead, and the power of mojo—the placing of curses, hexes, and death wishes by the use of ritualistic magic.

Clairvius Narcisse, the Most Famous "Zombie"

The most important person in some Haitian communities, especially remote settlements that have little contact with the major cities of the island, is the *bokor*—a Voodoo priest or black magician. Many Haitians live in fear of the *bokor*, who is considered a very powerful man never to be crossed. Whether or not you believe in Voodoo, there are some very good reasons to be afraid of the *bokor* because, in one form or another, zombies do exist, and to become one fits perfectly the cliché of "a fate worse than death."

According to believers, a zombie is the resurrected body of a dead person—someone who has been reconstituted by a *bokor* in order to perform a specific task. Practitioners of Voodoo claim that the *bokor* is able to capture the soul or spirit of a dead person and separate it from the body. The spirit is then contained in a special jar, and the body of the deceased is used for whatever purpose the priest chooses. To the believers, this is a purely supernatural process heavily dependent upon the skill of the much-feared priest. A particularly famous case will serve to illustrate.

On May 2, 1962, a young man by the name of Clairvius Narcisse "died" in the Albert Schweitzer Hospital in the small town of Deschapelles. The cause of his "death" was a mystery, but he had developed a fever a few days earlier and then went into respiratory failure. Pronounced dead, he was buried within a few days. Then, eighteen years later, his younger sister Angelina was shopping in the market of her home village, l'Estère, when from behind her she heard a voice she immediately recognized. She turned, and to her utter amazement saw a man she thought was long dead, her brother, Clairvius.

When she had calmed down and taken the man—who seemed confused and incoherent—back to his family, the story of his past eighteen years gradually came out.

His memory was hazy, but he recalled the scenes in the hospital almost two decades earlier. He remembered being short of breath and then slipping into a trancelike state. He could hear people talking and a doctor proclaiming him dead, but he had been unable to move or to say anything. It had been literally a living nightmare.

Checked by two doctors, one an American, the exact cause of Clairvius's condition was never ascertained, but because his skin was chalk-white and his heartbeat had slowed to an imperceptible rate, he had been pronounced dead and subsequently prepared for burial.

Clairvius remembered the sound of the lid closing on his coffin. Thinking that he really was going to die this time, one of the nails banged into the coffin pierced his cheek, and he could hear his sister weeping. After that he lost all track of time until he saw a light shining down on his face. He felt himself being dragged out of his coffin, and then several men set upon him, beating him almost to death before he was dragged away.

For the next two years he had been kept as a slave in the wild northern region of the country. He had been drugged by the *bokor* and regularly abused by him and the landowner who had enslaved him. Then, one day, one of his zombie companions suddenly awoke from his trance and turned on the *bokor*, killing him. With the priest and controller dead, the effects of whatever was keeping them sedated began to wear off and the entire group of slaves escaped. Clairvius wandered the island for another sixteen years until one day he heard that his brother had died, and this prompted him to return home.

At first the family were mystified by his account, and especially the reason for Clairvius's decision to return when he had. But he explained that it had been his brother who paid the local *bokor* to turn him into a zombie in the first place. The reason? Clairvius had crossed him.

Clairvius was eventually integrated back into his home village and accepted by the people he had known so many years before. He even became something of a national celebrity, appearing on television shows, the first person to publicly claim they had once been a zombie.

To rational nonbelievers, this entire story clearly has little to do with spirits being captured or "undead" beings roaming the countryside of Haiti. But if Clairvius was not one of the "undead" what really happened to him? Who were the zombies he encountered and how had the *bokor* exerted such power? . . .

Zombie Powder

The chemical route to becoming a zombie is rather delicate and requires skilled use of very particular drugs. The *bokor* makes a powder called a *coup poudre*, the preparation of which is surrounded by ritual and hocus-pocus to add status to what is in essence a simple blend of a few potentially lethal chemicals.

According to ritual, the *coup poudre* must be produced in June. To prepare it, the priest needs one "thunderstone" or *pierre tonnerre*, which is a piece of rock that has been buried underground for one year before it is unearthed by the *bokor*. To this, add one human skull and assorted bones; two puffer fish (preferably female), one of which must be *crapaud de mer*, the "sea toad;" one sea snake (the *polychaete worm*); vegetable oil; a sprig of a plant called a *tcha-tcha*; half a dozen pods of *pois gratter*, otherwise known as "itching pea;" two blue agamont lizards; one big toad, *Bufo marinus;* and finally an assortment of tarantulas, white tree frogs, and various insects according to taste.

These ingredients are to be used in the following way: the sea snake is tied to the leg of the toad, the *Bufo marinus*. The two are then placed in a jar and buried. The toad is said to "die of rage," which, according to Voodoo lore, increases the power of the poison it secretes into the jar. At no time must the *bokor* touch any of the ingredients because some of the most potent elements can be carried through the skin and are deadly in concentrated form.

As the toad and the sea snake are doing their work, the *bokor* places the human skull in a fire with the thunderstone and a collection of other ingredients until the skull turns black. While this is being prepared, he grinds the vegetable and insect ingredients together and adds some shavings of the skull, taken before it was placed in the fire. The mixture should then be ground to a fine powder along with the skull and thunderstone and the poison exuded by the toad. The entire mixture is then placed in a coffin underground for three days. This is even more potent if the coffin is the one containing the body from which the skull was removed to begin the process.

After three days, the *coup poudre* is ready. Traditionally, this is sprinkled in the shape of a cross on the doorstep of the targeted victim, but for a better chance of success it is more usually poured down the back or surreptitiously placed in a sock or shoe. The poison is then absorbed through the skin. Within hours the victim will have problems breathing, and will appear to "die" soon after.

The active ingredients in this ceremony boil down to just two components. First, the mix contains a chemical called *tetrodotoxin,* which comes from the female puffer fish. This is both an anesthetic and a poison. As an anesthetic, it is estimated to be almost 200,000 times more powerful than cocaine, and as a poison 500 times more deadly than cyanide. The other essential ingredient is another powerful anesthetic and hallucinogenic drug contained in the poisonous excretions of the *Bufo marinus,* a chemical called *bufotenine.*

Combined, these two compounds make a potentially lethal cocktail. In precisely the right doses, the preparation of which requires great skill, it can create the onset symptoms that make the victim appear to be dying. They go into a trancelike state, their breathing becomes so shallow it is almost undetectable, and they take on a deathly white pallor. This effect appears even more pronounced in hospitals such as those on Haiti (especially at the time Clairvius Narcisse was zombified in 1962), where highly sophisticated heart monitors are comparatively rare.

The rest of the components of the preparation are largely for ritualistic purposes, and their use has been refined over centuries primarily to add an element of the macabre and to instill greater fear into the minds of naïve country Haitians and those who want to believe.

The Living Dead

So, with the first stage over, we now have someone presumed dead but actually clinging onto life with barely perceptible life signs. They are duly buried, grieved over, and left in peace. It is then that the *bokor* and his helpers return to their work.

The next stage of the process requires the reanimation of the "dead" victim. Again, this is in part a delicate operation requiring precise timing. If the victim is left buried alive for too long, he really will die, but if he's dug up at precisely the right time, he will be usable. Which, incidentally, implies an almost unimaginable degree of cruelty on the part of those who pay for the *bokor*'s services. Not content with having someone killed, they employ the priest to make their enemy one of the "living dead."

Returning to the graveyard, the *bokor* and his team remove the victim's coffin and lift out the limp body. Next, they viciously beat them up. This might seem like unnecessary cruelty, and it is, but there are two reasons for it. The occult reason given by the *bokor* is that they have to make sure that the zombie's "will," the *ti bon ange*, is trapped and cannot return to the body, so that the victim is under the complete control of the priest. Sometimes, a *bokor* will add an extra nasty twist to this scenario. If he and his helpers are feeling particularly cruel (or they have been paid extra), instead of trapping the *ti bon ange* in a jar, they will endeavor to transpose it into the body of an insect. According to the Voodoo faith, in this way the *bokor* is almost certain to destroy the victim's chance of resurrection and eventual union with God. In effect, he is not only keeping a "dead body" alive, but destroying the very soul of the poor victim.

In purely biological terms, the beating is necessary because the bufotenine that has put the victim into an hallucinogenic trance can have unpredictable side effects, and sometimes the intoxicated zombie can go literally berserk. The beating has the effect of sedating them just as the effects of the tetrodotoxin may be wearing off.

In this state, the zombie is of little use to anyone. However, the job of removing the person from the community has been fulfilled and the *bokor* has already earned his fee. But he has more work to do if he wants to earn a further fee for turning the zombie into a compliant slave via the use of another cocktail of chemicals.

After the beating, the victim is led to a cross and baptized with a new name. This is usually something insulting and humiliating. He is then force-fed a paste made from sweet potato, cane syrup, and a drug called *datura stramonium*, commonly known as zombie's cucumber. Datura is another hallucinogen that causes psychotic delirium. It also contains a drug called *atropine*, which is the antidote for tetrodotoxin. So, this new chemical mix brings the zombie out of the catatonic state induced by the *coup poudre* and places him in a state of constant psychotic delirium, a bit like a permanent LSD trip in which the victim is able to walk, to carry out simple tasks such as working in a field, to eat and to drink. But zombies are unable to focus on reality, they cannot speak, and only understand vaguely what is happening to them.

As reported by Clairvius Narcisse, there have been cases where a zombie has snapped out of this condition, usually because the landowner to whom the zombies are enslaved forgets to administer the drugs at the appropriate time or erroneously allows the zombies certain forbidden foods. Most important of these is salt. At no time should zombies be allowed salt, because, according to tradition, this will allow them to return to the real world. This probably has something to do with the metabolic breakdown of the datura. Large quantities of salt will metabolize the drug into a less potent form, and the delirium will gradually slip away as a result. Understandably enraged, the zombie, who is more often than not a disreputable individual or criminal, will then turn on their keepers and murder them before escaping.

This scenario accounts for the way in which the vast majority of zombies have been produced by *bokors* in Haiti. No one knows how many people have been zombified, but over the centuries it may run into many thousands. It is thought that people in this state do not usually live very long; they are worked hard and the constant application of hallucinogenic drugs severely damages the brain, leading eventually to cerebral hemorrhaging and true death. . . .

However zombies are formed, the threat of zombification is very real in the minds of many Haitians. Sometimes families deliberately mutilate the bodies of their dead relatives just before burial to render them useless as slaves even if the *bokor* resurrects them. And, throughout their time as leaders of Haiti, the Duvaliers, "Papa Doc" Francois and "Baby Doc" Jean-Claude, regularly employed Voodoo imagery and occult ideas while officially outlawing its practice. Papa Doc even went so far as to let it be known that he was a powerful *bokor*, and he named his personal guards, his private mafia, *tontons macoutes* after the most powerful of Voodoo sorcerers. Although Baby Doc was deposed in 1986, a belief in Voodoo was never dented by the Duvalier's strictures and lives on after Haiti's former rulers have disappeared utterly from the political scene.

Mojo Rising

The other major aspect of Voodoo to be considered is the black art of harming or even killing victims by suggestion, by action at a distance using ritualistic black magic. This is the art of mojo.

Mojo is a curse or magic spell to bring harm to others. The traditional idea is of a Voodoo priest sticking pins in waxen images of the victim, which produce excruciating pain or even death. But there are other methods employed by various practitioners of black magic around the world. The aborigines use a technique called "bone-pointing" which involves no physical contact with the victim. Instead, during a carefully contrived ritualistic ceremony, a priest merely points a special bone at the victim and they are treated by the others as though they are already dead. Soon they are ostracized by the community, and often despair leads to suicide. Other priests use wooden effigies, the power of the magic enhanced by applying curses over cuttings of hair or nail clippings taken from the victim.

Again, to many Haitians this is a very real and potent aspect of their faith. When American marines landed on Haiti during a brief occupation of the island in 1994, it was widely believed that there were groups of *bokors* working to thwart the military effort by the use of curses and hexes. The same year, an American judge actually jailed a man on Haiti whom he believed was preparing a curse against him because this well-known voodoo priest had been found mixing a lock of the judge's hair into a specially prepared elixir.

Quite naturally, emotive rituals such as those performed by Voodoo priests are easily exaggerated by believers and practitioners alike. The believers want to believe and are fearful, and the priests are manipulating hysteria and anxiety for their own ends. As a result, there is no shortage of graphic tales that appear superficially to support fantastic claims that there is real magic at work when the priest points a bone or impales an image with a needle.

During the 1930s the anthropologist Dr. Herbert Basedow was one of the first to introduce Europeans to stories of priests applying the black arts and conjuring the evil of mojo. He included what was then a startling account of such a ritual in a book about aboriginal tribes called *The Australian Aboriginal*. In it he wrote:

> A man who discovers that he is being boned by an enemy is, indeed, a pitiable sight. He stands aghast, with his eyes staring at the treacherous pointer, with his hands lifted as though to ward off the lethal medium, which he imagines is pouring into his body. His cheeks blanch and his eyes become glassy, and the expression of his face becomes horribly distorted . . . he attempts to shriek, but usually the sound chokes in his throat, and all one might see is froth at his mouth. His body begins to tremble and the muscles twist involuntarily. He sways backwards and falls to the ground, and for a short time appears to be in a swoon; but soon after he begins to writhe as if in mortal agony, and covering his face with his hands, begins to moan. After a while he becomes more composed and crawls to his wurley [his hut]. From this time onward he sickens and frets, refusing to eat and keeping aloof from the daily affairs of the tribe. Unless help is forthcoming in the shape of a counter-charm, administered by the hands of the *Nangarri* or medicine man, his death is only the matter of a comparatively short time. If the coming of the medicine man is opportune, he might be saved.

As with the zombification of victims, there are two crucial elements in this series of events that go some way to explaining how such seemingly grotesque and frightening phenomena could occur. The first is the fact that the victim is almost invariably a troublemaker. This entire ritual can be interpreted as a court dishing out a punishment. These people live in small isolated communities in which the only law is that the strong dominate the weak. Equally, in some cases, those hurt by a troublesome member of the community can rely upon the medicine man to intervene. The "victim" in the above account is basically ostracized by everyone he knows and falls into a deep depression. This is fueled by guilt and the fear of the medicine man, a fear that has been instilled into the members of the community since early childhood.

The other factor to consider is the liberal use of hallucinogenic drugs. Although Basedow made no specific mention of this in his account, it is well-known that most tribal people around the globe use some form of drug as recreation and for ritualistic purposes, whether it be alcohol, mescaline, or other less well-known but often very powerful agents. In a situation involving a combination of drugs and the power of a community turning on an individual, there should be little surprise that the effect is very powerful indeed.

This potent blend should not be underestimated. The ethnobiologist Wade Davis has suggested that the victim of a hex actually becomes a threat to the community and that the community actively conspires in the eventual death of that victim. In some cases, they deliberately mourn in front of the victim, as though he were already dead.

The "Giving-Up Complex"

This conspiracy activates and encourages what scientists have dubbed a "giving-up complex." They describe this as being similar to the frame of mind sometimes adopted by people who suffer from terminally ill disease—they "lose the will to live." It is easy to imagine how anyone could adopt the giving-up complex after a terrifying ceremony in which they are cursed and have their former friends and family treating them as if they were already dead; especially if this treatment is combined with the use of mind-altering drugs.

Wade Davis describes this as a form of "total social rejection." He says, "Although physically the victim still lives, psychologically he is dying, and socially *he is already dead.*"

Crucial to the success of this process is total belief in what is happening both within the mind of the victim and in the community as a whole. Professor Gottlieb Freisinger of the Johns Hopkins University in Baltimore has declared that, "special circumstances and beliefs in a community must exist before an individual can die by hex." And psychologist Stanford Cohen, working at Boston University, believes that "hexing can be fatal when it implants a mixture of fear and helplessness in the victim."

Wade Davis rightly points out: "Even doctors of the most traditional sort admit the role psychology plays on our well being." And: "If one believes strongly enough then it is more likely to happen."

To demonstrate that the power of suggestion is greatly influenced by the total commitment to a belief in what is happening, Professor William Sargent, an expert in brainwashing techniques, used electric-shock therapy on a woman who was convinced she was being cursed. He persuaded the woman that the electric shocks had removed the hex, and she duly recovered.

But is this the entire answer? Surely there are some individuals who would be resilient to the pressure of those around them? This may be true, especially if we consider that many of the so-called victims of hexes are themselves actually unpleasant individuals, including in their number thieves, murderers, and rapists, or those who have crossed others seriously enough to have become subject to the attention of the medicine man. But no matter how tough they may be, they would face serious practical problems because of the treatment of the community.

Firstly, if the community is treating the victim as though they were already dead then presumably the hexed individual would find it hard to continue daily life, to eat or drink, to find shelter or gainful employment. Their only option would then be to leave, but they would probably be prevented from doing so. Inevitably their health would suffer and they would fall into rapid decline. But even then, there may be purely biochemical reasons for hastening this fall.

During the 1920s, doctors treating soldiers who had returned shell-shocked from the trenches, discovered a new syndrome precipitated by a process called, *vagal inhibition.* This is caused by an over-stimulation of the adrenal system. If the blood is flooded with adrenaline, the blood supply to the extremities of the body is reduced so that blood can be concentrated in the muscles. The reason for this is simple: Adrenaline is pumped into the body to stimulate the muscles ready for "fight or flight." However, with the supply of blood to the extemities reduced, the cells in these parts of the body become less infused with oxygen and the tiny capillaries that carry blood (and oxygen) to these regions become more permeable to blood plasma. The blood plasma then seeps into the tissue surrounding the capillaries further reducing blood pressure.

This vicious circle of events causes a continued drop in blood pressure and if left unchecked, the victim will die. The process takes a few days and is almost certainly a major factor in the gradual "fading-away" so often described in mojo stories.

So, it appears that the ability of bokor to produce the "undead" and the power of the medicine man or the priest to cause the death of someone by suggestion are both real and powerful phenomena. However, neither are "supernatural"—each can be explained using the accepted laws of science. In the case of the zombification of victims, the bokor utilizes a complex amalgam of drugs mixed with ancient rituals to generate fear in the community over which he commands a powerful position. The use of mojo, or hexes is a blend of sociological factors, that work strongly against the victim, combined with the liberal use of drugs. In each case, fear lies at the heart of the ritual and the practice. In the case of hexing, this element of fear may be the crucial factor that sets in motion an elaborate chain of biochemical events ending in death.

In Haiti there is a proverb that sums up precisely the many-layered complexities of this ancient, elemental and highly devisive religion. It says: "The closer you get to Voodoo, the more vulnerable you are to its power." A scientific explanation for the work of the *bokor* does nothing to diminish the truth and the power of this aphorism.

Most Zombies Are Cases of Mistaken Identity

Roland Littlewood and Chavannes Douyon

In 1997 researchers Roland Littlewood and Chavannes Douyon conducted a study on three individuals found wandering in remote Haitian villages. Each of the three was believed by locals to be a long-lost relative who had been poisoned for unknown reasons by a malevolent witch doctor, buried alive, and enslaved as a zombie for a number of years before somehow escaping captivity. The researchers' findings, which follow, suggest that all three subjects were simply victims of mental disorders and mistaken by aggrieved relatives for missing loved ones to whom they bore a passing resemblance. Roland Littlewood is a professor of psychiatry and anthropology at University College London. Chavannes Douyon is a professor of psychology at the Polyclinic Medica in Port-au-Prince, Haiti.

Zombification became a subject of popular Western interest during the occupation of Haiti by the USA between 1915 and 1934.[1] The current United Nations intervention has again focused attention on a phenomenon regarded as exotic and improbable by the media, yet one which is taken by most Haitians as empirically verifiable. Along with the related religious practice of vodu, it has been implausibly related by US physicians to the current epidemic of AIDS in Haiti.[2] Haitian medical practitioners regard zombification as the consequence of poisoning; the clergy as the product of sorcery. Zombis are frequently recognised by the local population, and estimates of their number are of the order of up to a thousand new cases per year (LP Mars, personal communication).

Zombification is a crime under the Haitian Penal Code (Article 246) where it is considered as murder although the zombified individual is still alive. Local interpretation is that either by poisoning or sorcery, a young person suddenly and inexplicably becomes ill, is subsequently recognised by their family as dead, placed in a tomb, stolen by a boko (sorcerer) in the next few days, and secretly returned to life and activity but not to full awareness and agency.[3,4] Haitians are seldom buried but placed in painted concrete family tombs above ground which in country areas are on family land next to the houses; they are vulnerable to being broken open.

Local beliefs about body, mind, and spirit recognise a separation of the corps cadavre (physical body) with its gwobon anj (animating principle) from the ti-bon anj (agency, awareness, and memory).[3-5] In zombification, the latter is retained by the sorcerer, usually in a fastened bottle or earthenware jar where it is known as the zombi astral. The boko either extracts it through sorcery which leaves the victim apparently dead, or else captures it after a natural death before it has gone too far from the body.[1,3,4] The animated body remains without will or agency as the zombi cadavre, which becomes the slave of the boko and works secretly on his land or is sold to another boko for the same purpose. It is induced to remain a slave only through chaining and beating, or through further poisoning and sorcery. This zombi cadavre is the zombie popularised by Western cinema and indeed is referred to locally by that name. In Haiti, the term is also used in metaphor to refer to extreme passivity and control by another.

Ingredients for Zombification

Explanations as to how a zombi cadavre may escape back to its original family suggest that either the bottle containing the zombi astral breaks; or the boko inadvertently feeds his zombi salt; or he dies and the zombi is liberated by his family; or, rarely, the zombi may be released through divine intervention. On release, their mental and physical status remains the same, and they are vulnerable to recapture and continued enslavement; few bokos or doctors claim to be able to return a zombi cadavre to its original state of health and agency, and the matter is reserved for the mercy of Le Grand Maitre (the rather remote God recognised by vodu practitioners who is only invoked briefly through Latin prayers before they begin their ceremonies). Zombis are recognised by their fixed staring expression, their nasal intonation (which they share with manifestations of the spirits of the dead); by repeated, purposeless, and clumsy actions; and by limited and repetitive speech. They are regarded with commiseration; fear is reserved for the possibility of being zombified oneself. Concern that a deceased relative may be vulnerable to zombification justifies prevention through decapitation of the corpse before burial, or poisons and charms placed in the coffin.

Anthropological accounts of zombification usually just detail local explanations[3] or follow them to explain sorcery as a psycho-social or biological phenomenon.[1-5] There has been medical interest in the possibility that zombification may be an empirical state—catalepsy or motor paralysis—which is induced by neurotoxins followed by retrieval and revival of the "dead" person extracted from the tomb.[5,6] Among the poisons which have been implicated is tetrodotoxin (from the puffer fishes Sphoeroides testudineus and Diodon hystrix) with Datura stramonium used to revive and then control the zombi.[5,6] Tetrodotoxin has been studied biomedically in Japan where the puffer fish is a delicacy whose consumption may result in apparent but temporary death.[6,7] Other ingredients mentioned by Haitian bokos as zombifacients include human remains, a polychaete worm, toads, lizards, and tarantulas.[5] No in-vivo research has been carried out with the suggested toxins, and whilst Haitian medical practitioners are familiar with the phenomenon of zombification,[8] they have not published its clinical characteristics. Studies of the one well-documented instance of a returned zombi[5,8] concentrated on his symptoms at the time of presumed death, little on his mental and physical state at the time of the post-return interview (although a lay observer[9] did not remark any abnormality at this interview). Another well-known case who was hospitalised has been argued as an instance of mistaken identity.[1,4] Local doctors suggest that zombification can be recognised only by the absence of any characteristic features of mental illness and by verbal and motor preservation. Do zombis manifest any characteristic clinical pattern? Are they the deceased individuals their relatives claim to recognise?

FI

Three cases of zombification in southern Haiti in 1996–97 were examined in their homes and their histories taken from relatives and others in Creole. The temporary presence of a private computed tomography scanner from the Dominican Republic allowed two of them to be taken to Port-au-Prince to be scanned. To avoid mistaken identity by a bereaved relative, DNA samples were obtained in two instances. Local bokos who practised zombification were asked to comment on the cases.

FI was around 30 years old when she died after a short febrile illness and was buried by her family the same day in the family tomb next to her house. 3 years later she was recognised by a friend wandering near the village; her mother confirmed her identity by a facial mark, as did her 7-year-old daughter, her siblings, other villagers, her husband, and the local priest. She appeared mute and unable to feed herself. Her parents accused her husband of zombifying her (he was jealous of her after she had had an affair). After a local court authorised the opening of her tomb, which was full of stones, her parents were undecided whether to take her home and she was admitted to the psychiatric hospital in Port-au-Prince.

On examination, she looked much younger and thinner than in an earlier family photograph. She kept her head in a lowered position, and walked extremely slowly and stiffly, barely moving her arms. On examination, her muscles had reduced tone, but there was no waxy flexibility. Apparently lacking motivation and unable to signal any wishes, she did not reply to questions but would occasionally murmur some incomprehensible but stereotyped words, and was indifferent to passing events. She required assistance to feed herself. Electroencephalogram and central nervous system examination were unremarkable. She did not co-operate with a psychological assessment, nor with attempts at social rehabilitation. She did not respond to neuroleptics. On being taken to a market for an outing, she was immediately recognised by the crowd as a zombi.

The presumptive diagnosis was catatonic schizophrenia (which is locally a not uncommon psychiatric illness[10]).

WD

WD, 26 years old, was the eldest son of an alleged former tonton macoute (secret policeman) under the Duvaliers' regime. The father was our principal informant together with WD's mother and other villagers. When he was 18, he suddenly became ill with a fever, "his eyes turned yellow," he "smelled bad like death," and "his body swelled up". Suspecting sorcery, his father asked his older brother to obtain advice from a boko, but WD died after 3 days and was buried in a tomb on family land next to the house of a female cousin. The tomb was not, as was customary, watched that night. 19 months later, WD reappeared at a nearby cock fight, recognised his father, and accused his uncle of zombifying him. He correctly recalled comments made by his family at the funeral. He was recognised as a zombi by the other villagers, the local Catholic priest, and the magistrate. He remained at his father's house, his legs secured to a log to stop him wandering away. His uncle was arrested at his father's request and sentenced by the provincial court to life imprisonment for zombification, confessing that he had been jealous of his brother who had used his literacy to register all the family land in his own name. WD's father's story was supported by the villagers, the judges and priest involved in the court case, the local coffin maker, and by examination of WD's death certificate and the proceedings of the uncle's trial. The uncle escaped from prison during the political turmoil of 1991. We traced him and he agreed to an interview in exchange for protection. He denied sorcery or poisoning, saying the case was a trick on the part of WD's father to expropriate his property entirely, and his confession had been induced through torture by the police. The female cousin denied involvement in WD's zombification but refused to allow us to open the tomb on her land.

WD was a slightly built man, constantly scowling, looking younger than his age, much thinner than in an old photograph his parents showed us. He spent most of his time sitting or lying in a characteristic position, lower limbs to the left, upper limbs to the right, rarely speaking spontaneously and only in single words which were normal in form and content. He could not describe his period of burial or enslavement but agreed he was malad (ill) and a zombi. He could be persuaded to walk with normal posture and gait, steadily but slowly. His parents reported that he was not incontinent and would tell them when he was hungry, but they had to bathe him and change his clothes. His eyes scanned around him with clear intent, his hands picking aimlessly at his nails or at the ground, and he avoided eye contact. His wrists were scarred all around, consistent with abrasions caused by chains or wire. A hyperextended fourth finger was identified by his mother as the consequence of a childhood accident. There was a small circular hole, 5 mm in diameter with scar tissue over his sternum which occasionally oozed pus and which had been present since his return; his father said he thought this was where poison had been administered to keep him quiescent during his 18 months of slavery. General and central nervous system examination was unremarkable except for slight muscle wasting. He had difficulty identifying familiar objects when placed unseen in his hand, but would name them when he saw them. His parents reported periods of anger and irritation when he would ineffectually hit and kick out at others generally after being teased, and malkadi (fits) during his sleep about once a week when he would cry out and his limbs would go into rigid spasm. There [was] no evident thought disorder, hallucinations, or catatonia.

The presumptive diagnosis was organic brain syndrome and epilepsy consistent with a period of anoxia [oxygen deficiency]. His fits reduced to once a month with phenytoin 100 mg per day.

MM

MM, aged 31, was the younger sister of our principal informant who described her as formerly a friendly but quiet and shy girl, not very bright. At the age of 18, MM had joined some friends in prayers for a neighbour who had been zombified; she herself then became ill with diarrhoea and fever, her body swelled up and she died in a few days. The family suspected revenge sorcery. After 13 years, MM had reappeared in the town market 2 months before we met her, with an account of having been kept as a zombi in a village 100 miles to the north, and having borne a child to another zombi (or perhaps to the boko). On the death of the boko, his son had released her and she travelled home on foot. Her brother, a nominal Catholic had converted to his own version of evangelical Protestantism. On his sister's return, he recognised her as a zombi and started a daily healing service involving the rest of the family and friends in glossolalia and laying on of hands.

MM looked younger than her age, with a small head and ears, thin and slightly built. She readily responded to attention, asked questions spontaneously, giggled frequently, and laughed inappropriately. General, central nervous system, and mental state examination were unremarkable except for a round sternal scar 1 cm in diameter. Her speech was fairly limited but appropriate with grammatical short sentences. She agreed she was ill but not that she was a zombi. She was not regarded by her neighbours as a typical zombi because of her resonant affect and responsiveness to others. Her brother said she was duller (pa-intelijan) than she had been formerly. She was not able to sign her name and appeared to us to be of low intelligence. She readily gave a vague account of her imprisonment which agreed with that given by her brother. Her self-care was normal but her family reported that she enjoyed being cared for and cuddled. Our presumptive diagnosis was learning disability, perhaps fetal alcohol syndrome.

With MM's agreement, we took her to the area where she said she had been kept as a zombi. She was immediately recognised in the market as a local woman known to be simple who had been enticed away 9 months previously by a band of rara musicians during the lenten carnival. Both families now insisted that MM was theirs and accused the other family of zombification. MM's daughter and brother then appeared, who closely resembled her in physical appearance, mannerisms, suggestibility, and minor learning disability. She recognised her daughter whom she had previously named correctly to us but she still insisted its father was a fellow zombi. The villagers said she had been formerly married to a local man but we were unable to locate him. MM appeared to recognise her cousin as the boko's son, but the villagers ridiculed the idea.

We assumed that MM's case was one of mistaken identity. She had apparently been abducted, or wandered away from her home and eventually ended up where she was recognised as a deceased and now zombified sister.

Conclusions

We interviewed two sorcerers and attended the pilay fey (sorcery protection) ceremonies of the first. Like most sorcerers, he had his own temple as well as being the convenor of one of the secret societies (zobop, bizango, cochon gris, secte rouge) which have been implicated in zombification[5,7] and which are illegal under sections 224 and 227 of the Penal Code. The second boko had converted to Protestant evangelism, is now a well-known opponent of vodu, and holds dramatic church meetings at which he gives lurid accounts of his past sorcery. Neither had been implicated in the above cases; both knew the other by reputation and maintained surprisingly cordial relations. They agreed the cases we described were plausible, and they recognised as part of their own pharmacoepia both a puffer fish and a branch of Hippomane mancinella (zombi apple, manchineel) which we supplied and which is commonly cited as the astringent used by a sorcerer in topical application of a poison.[9]. . .

DNA fingerprinting[11] suggested that WD was not the son of his putative parents; nor was MM related to either of the men who claimed to be her brothers, but she was likely to be the mother of the child whom she said was her daughter.

Computed tomograph scans on WD and MM were within normal limits.

It is unlikely that there is a single explanation for all zombis. Mistaken identification of a wandering, mentally ill, stranger by bereaved relatives is the most likely explanation[4]—as in the cases of MM and WD. People with a chronic schizophrenic illness, brain damage, or learning disability are not uncommonly met with wandering in Haiti, and they would be particularly likely to be identified as lacking volition and memory which are characteristics of a zombi. Interpretations of mental illness as an alienation of some vital faculty of agency are common in Central America and in the Caribbean.[12] The ready local recognition of zombis, as with MM, and their generally considerate treatment might be seen as an institutionalised restitution of the destitute mentally ill: recognition and incorporation of a zombi into a family provides public recognition and sometimes material advantage. What is more difficult to understand is the apparent acquiescence of the "returned relative" not only to being a zombi but to being a "relative".

The local understanding that the unexpected death of a young adult is never a properly natural death (mo bondiay),[12,13] together with the frequency of sorcery suspicions and the number of people who told us they were engaged in attempts at zombification, suggest the breaking open of tombs by bokos is widespread. The use of human remains in sorcery is so common that most country tombs have been broken into, and the majority of oufos (temples) we examined contained human skulls and other body parts. Given that death is locally recognised without access to medical certification, and that burial usually occurs within a day of death, it is not implausible for a retrieved person to be alive. The use of Datura stramonium to revive them, and its possible repeated administration during the period of zombi slavery, could produce a state of extreme psychological passivity.

We cannot exclude the use of a neuromuscular toxin, topically administered together with a local irritant by a boko, to induce catalepsy followed by secret retrieval of the poisoned individual.[5] Japanese evidence of tetrodotoxin poisoning indicates that a full and rapid recovery can occur spontaneously.[7] This would presumably be consistent with the history of FI who could have suffered anoxic brain damage in the tomb.

That bokos actually enslave zombis on secret agricultural grounds is implausible given the high population density of Haiti. Zombis have never been identified in captivity but only on their return. Under the Duvaliers who mobilised the oungans as their secret police,[15] and in the lengthy period of political terror, social instability, and economic blockade during and after the Duvalier regime,[9,15] there were numerous cases of abduction, torture, sexual slavery, and secret homicide cloaked in vodu maintained by state terror and suspicions of sorcery.[15,16]

A fuller consideration of zombification would require an analysis of Haitian identity and of the wider political articulations of village-level conflict and sorcery accusation. It would be interesting to know how the zombi reflects not only local understanding of psychopathology but Haiti's national history as the black republic[17,18] of former slaves who have continued to face the ever-present threat of political dependency, external intervention, and loss of self-determination.[16,18,19]

References

1. Hurston ZN. Voodoo gods. London: Dent, 1938.

2. Farmer P. Aids and accusation: Haiti and the geography of blame. Berkeley: University of California Press, 1992.

3. Metraux A. Le vaudou haitien. Paris: Gallimard, 1958.

4. Mars LP. The story of zombi in Haiti. Man 1945; 45: 38–40.

5. Davis W. Passage of darkness: the ethnobiology of the Haitian zombie. Chapel Hill: University of North Carolina Press, 1988.

6. Anon. Puffers, gourmands and zombification (editorial). Lancet 1984; ii: 1220–21.

7. Torda TA, Sinclair E, Ulyatt DB. Puffer fish (tetrodotoxin) poisoning: clinical records and suggested management. Med J Austral 1973; 1: 599–602.

8. Douyon L. Les zombis dans le contexte vodu et haitien. Haiti Sante 1980; 2:19–23.

9. Thomson I. Bonjour blanc. London: Hutchinson, 1992.

10. Douyon L. Introduction aux traitements des malades mentaux en Haiti. Bull Centre Psychiat Neurol 1972; 11: 5–8.

11. Jeffreys AT, Wilson A, Thein SL. Individual-specific 'fingerprints' of human DNA. Nature 1985; 316: 76–79.

12. Littlewood R. Pathology and identity: the work of Mother Earth in Trinidad. Cambridge: Cambridge University Press, 1993.

13. Brodwin P. Medicine and morality in Haiti: the contest for healing power. Cambridge: Cambridge University Press, 1996.

14. Diederich B, Burt A. Papa Doc: Haiti and its dictator. Harmondsworth: Penguin, 1972.

15. Aristide JB. Tout homme est un homme, tout moun se moun. Paris: Seuil, 1993.

16. Human Rights Watch. Thirst for justice: a decade of impunity in Haiti. New York: HRW, 1996.

17. St John S. Hayti or the black republic. London: Smith, Elder and Co., 1884.

18. Nicholls D. From Dessalines to Duvalier: race, colour and national independence in Haiti. Cambridge: Cambridge University Press, 1979.

19. Larose S. The meaning of Africa in Haitian vodu. In: Lewis IM, ed. Symbols and Sentiments. London: Academic Press, 1977.

Some Scientists Reject the Existence of Zombie Drugs

William Booth

Wade Davis achieved fame and fortune with two memoirs documenting his infiltration of the Haitian underworld and his contention that zombies are real, if not supernaturally generated. The second of Davis's books, *Passage of Darkness*, featured detailed analysis of the compounds used to make "zombie powder." One drug enables the voodoo priest to poison his victim into a simulation of death. After the victim is buried, the voodoo priest digs the victim up and uses a second drug to resuscitate him for use as a slave. Here journalist William Booth compares Davis's testimony with that of several leading pharmacologists and raises questions concerning Davis's scientific methods, specifically whether Davis falsified or misreported chemical analyses to bolster his case. Booth also examines the ethics of Davis's ordering zombie powder through underworld channels, which theo-

William Booth, "Voodoo Science," *Science*, vol. 240, April 15, 1988, p. 274.

retically would have involved the illegal exhumation of at least one human corpse.

Ａ young botanist from Harvard University named Wade Davis claims to have discovered a pharmacological explanation for zombies, the "living dead" of Haitian folklore. But his detractors say his assertions are bunk and his methods are unscientific.

The lingering controversy has been sparked in part by the collision of two different worlds of research. In the first world, the intrepid ethnobotanist Davis goes down to the troubled island nation of Haiti. His mission: discover how zombies are made. What Davis found was "a surrealistic landscape" and a country "full of spirits." Armed with cash but scant knowledge of Haitian Creole, Davis immersed himself in the secret societies of the voodoo religion. With sorcerers as paid informants, Davis participated in the preparation of several batches of "zombies powder", and witnessed the exhumation of the corpse of a child from a rural graveyard at night. When Davis emerged from his trials in Haiti, he reported having found the pharmacological under-pinning for the zombie phenomenon. Fame and fortune followed.

This romantic world has collided with another world, a less glamorous place of mass spectrometers, gas chromatography, and mouse bioassays, where a group of toxicologists and pharmacologists familiar with the work of Davis are crying foul. Leading the charge is C.Y. Kao of State University of New York Downstate Medical Center in Brooklyn, who has aggressively challenged Davis at every turn. Kao does not mince words: "I actually feel this is an issue of fraud in science." One of Kao's comrades in the dispute, Bo Holmstedt of the Karolinska Institute in Stockholm, is more restrained: "It is not deliberate fraud. It is withholding negative data. It is simply bad science."

The controversy involves the role of a powerful poison called tetrodotoxin in the creation of zombies. Davis' critics say there is either no tetrododoxin or little in the samples of zombies powder brought back by Davis to support his hypothesis. But there is more to it than that. The pharmacologists are accusing Davis of not playing by the rules by suppressing information that fails to bolster his case, while playing up a number of unconfirmed experiments that are repeatedly cited in his work as "personal communications." Some of the critics seem especially irked because Davis sought out their assistance but allegedly refuses to listen when told his conclusions are not supported by the evidence. "I feel like I've been taken for a ride," says Kao.

Trips to Haiti

The story is complicated by the popular accounts of Davis and the sensational nature of his work. Predictably, there have been a flurry of articles and television programs, for who does not enjoy a good story about zombies now and then? Davis also wrote a popular book in 1985 called *The Serpent and the Rainbow* and then sold the rights to Hollywood, which . . . released a rather lurid movie under the same title. Another book about zombies—this time a scholarly treatment based almost entirely on Davis' Harvard dissertation—is scheduled for release in May [1988] by the University of North Carolina Press. All of this attention has certainly created bad feelings, with pronouncements from both sides becoming increasingly invidious. Davis says that Kao and others are victims of "old-fashioned jealousy."

The story begins in 1982, when Davis was introduced to the late Nathan Kline, then director of the Rockland State

Research Institute in New York. Kline, a pioneer in the use of tranquilizers, wanted Davis to go to Haiti to search for a mysterious powder reputedly used to make zombies. Despite 30 years of work in Haiti, Kline had never succeeded in securing such a sample.

When Davis met Kline, the older man was particularly excited about zombies because he and a colleague in Haiti believed that for the first rime they had found a verifiable case, a man named Clairvius Narcisse, who returned to his village after an 18-year absence, claiming to have been made a zombie and sold into slavery. Narcisse has since become quite famous as the object of documentaries by the BBC and ABC. Narcisse's account, though highly intriguing, is far from watertight. Davis himself says that Narcisse had received so much attention by the time he arrived that the case was hard to evaluate. Other anthropologists with years of experience in Haiti discount the reality of zombies. "You hear stories all the time, but you can never actually find a zombie," says Leslie Desmangles of Trinity College in Hartford, Connecticut, a Haitian who has studied the religions of his homeland for the past 15 years.

Davis made several trips to Haiti between 1982 and 1984, collecting a total of eight samples of zombie powder from several voodoo sorcerers, or "bokors" as they are called. Most of the powders contained a variety of ingredients. Some included the fresh remains of a human cadaver, as well as stinging nettles, noxious toads, and one or more species of puffer fish found in Haitian waters. It was the fish that interested Davis, since puffer fish are known to sometimes contain the potent tetrodotoxin. Tetrodotoxin blocks the sodium channels between nerve endings and can cause paralysis and death. Davis says he paid about $300 for each sample, an enormous sum of money in Haiti, which is one of the poorer countries in the Western Hemisphere.

Davis' Powder

According to the hypothesis touted by Davis, the process of "zombification" works something like this: A victim is administered a powder that contains among other things the dried and pulverized remains of puffer fish, whose livers and reproductive organs may contain tetrodotoxin. At a dosage containing a precise amount of tetrodotoxin, Davis maintains that a victim of zombie powder poisoning could lapse into a state of such low metabolic activity that he might appear clinically dead. This poor soul would then be buried alive, only to be rescued hours later by a sorcerer who digs up the victim, feeds him an hallucinogenic paste, and then sells his newly minted zombie into slavery, often to sugar plantations.

As Davis points out, not all victims of tetrodotoxin poisoning would become zombies. A psychological or cultural predisposition is essential. One has to live in Haiti and believe in zombies to actually become one. It is what Davis calls the "set and setting" of the experience. For example, says Davis, a person who goes into the woods with the purpose of eating hallucinogenic mushrooms usually enjoys his experience. But the person who eats the mushrooms by mistake is often rushed to the emergency room, thinking himself a victim of poisoning.

Upon return to the United States after his first trip to Haiti in 1982, Davis provided several samples of zombie powder to Leon Roizin, a pathologist from Columbia Presbyterian Hospital in New York City who has been studying the effects of drugs on the central nervous system for 40 years. As a personal favor to his "old friend" Kline, Roizin agreed to test the crude mixtures on several rats and one rhesus monkey. He administered the zombie powder by rubbing an extract onto the shaved bellies of the rats or by injecting a solution into peritoneal tissue. What happened next was very intriguing. According to the account cited as a personal communication from Roizin to Davis, some rats "appeared comatose and showed no response at all to external stimuli. The electroencephalograph continued to monitor central nervous system activity, and the hearts were not affected. Certain rats remained immobilized for 24 hours and then recovered with no apparent sign of injury." A somewhat similar response was observed in the monkey.

Successive Experiments

Roizin is upset that the results of this preliminary experiment have been circulated by Davis. "I am very embarrassed," says Roizin, who maintains that he was promised by Kline that the powders would be thoroughly analyzed and that the initial experiment was "just among friends" to see if there was any biological activity. The experiment was never repeated by Roizin and has never been published. Roizin returned all trace of the powders and today refuses to have anything to do with Davis. "Wherever someone added some kind of drug, I don't know. How do I know that something was not added to that material?" says Roizin, who reports that he has produced catatonia and immobility in lab animals with other compounds, such as various neuroleptics, analgesics, and hallucinogens.

An experiment like Roizin's, however, was attempted again. In 1984, Davis and John Hartung, a Harvard anthropologist turned medical researcher at SUNY's Downstate Medical Center in Brooklyn, encouraged rats to ingest zombie powder by mixing it with peanut butter. They also rubbed the powder onto the rats' shaved bellies and injected powder in solution into the peritoneal cavities of mice and rats. "We failed completely," says Hartung. The animals did not become immobilized, let alone proto-zombies. Reports Hartung: "It is my suspicion that there was no tetrodotoxin in the samples we tested."

The experiment has never been published, and unlike Roizin's results, is not cited as a "Personal communication" by Davis. Hartung defends the silence, stating that "absence of evidence is not evidence of absence." It is a refrain repeated often by Davis and one that drives his critics to distraction. "What does that mean? The burden of proof is no longer on the scientist? Does it mean I can say anything I want and then tell my critics it is up to them to prove me wrong?" says John Moore, a physiologist at Duke University Medical Center in Durham who relayed Kao's charges to the University of North Carolina Press, publishers of Davis' new book.

Moving Target

Evidence that tetrodotoxin plays a central role in the initial phase of the zombification process has proved to be something of a moving target. No one disputes the observation by Davis that bokors add pulverized puffer fish to their zombie powders. What they dispute is the role of tetrodotoxin in transforming victims into the living dead. In Davis' first paper on the topic in 1983, he reported in the *Journal of Ethnopharmacology* that "the poisons which I collected during my first two expeditions to Haiti are currently being analyzed at the Karolinska Institute in Stockholm and at the University of Lausanne, Switzerland." Then Davis details the "initial experiments" of Roizin and suggests that "3.5 grams of crude poison might put a 73-kilogram human into a comatose, catalyptic state (Roizin, personal communication)." Davis concludes: "These preliminary laboratory results, together with what we know from the field and from the biomedical literature suggest strongly that there is an ethnopharmacological basis to the zombie phenomenon."

In his 1986 Ph.D. dissertation at Harvard, entitled "The ethnobiology of the Haitian zombie," Davis reported the details of Roizin's experiment, yet failed to [show] more [of] his own work with Hartung. As for further proof that tetrodotoxin helps make zombies, Davis wrote: "Laboratory tests have shown both the presence of tetrodotoxin in the samples, and have indicated that the powders when applied topically to rats and monkeys are biologically active." The citation is Davis' 1983 paper in *Journal of Ethnopharmacology*, which contains no evidence for the presence of tetrodotoxin. It also implies that tetrodotoxin was present in all of the samples, which is incorrect. To date, tetrodotoxin has only been found in one sample.

In his latest book, *Passage of Darkness: The Ethnobiology of the Haitian Zombie*, Davis again cites Roizin. In a footnote, Davis adds that "three distinct analytical techniques provided unequivocal evidence that tetrodotoxin is present in [one] sample." The citation is a personal communication from Laurent Rivier at the University of Lausanne.

Tracking the analysis of the various powders is an equally tricky business. The only published data appear in a letter to the journal *Toxicon* from Kao and Takeshi Yasumoto of the Tohoku University in Sendai, Japan. A well-known authority on tetrodotoxin, Kao received two samples of zombie powder from Davis in 1984. Initially very excited about the research, Kao did some preliminary assays on mice and found no biological activity, so he sent the samples to Yasumoto, who had developed an automated tetrodotoxin analyzer based on high-performance liquid chromatography (HPLC), a method which separates chemical components out of a solution. Kao says that he called upon Yasumoto for help because Yasumoto has been involved in testing the stomach contents of victims of fugu fish poisoning in Japan, where gourmands occasionally eat improperly prepared fugu, a species similar to the puffer fish identified by Davis as ingredients in zombie power. (Normally fugu should contain only enough tetrodotoxin to give diners tingling lips and a sense of mild euphoria, though sometimes the chef makes a tragic mistake.) Using his HPLC machine and mouse bioassays, Yasumoto found less than 1.1 micrograms of tetrodotoxin per gram of crude material in one sample. In the other sample, they found far less. Kao and Yasumoto called the amounts "insignificant traces." They wrote: "From these results it can be concluded that the widely circulated claim in the lay press to the effect that tetrodotoxin is the causal agent in the initial zombification process is without factual foundation."

At Lausanne, Rivier eventually received six samples of powder from Davis. In letters written in 1983 and 1985, Rivier informed Davis that little or no tetrodotoxin could be found. "I am rather disappointed by these results," Rivier wrote. In 1986, Rivier sent portions of all six samples to Michel Lazdunski, director of the Center for Biochemistry at the University of Nice in France. Using a competitive binding assay that involved radiolabeled tetrodotoxin and the sodium channels of rat brain membranes, Lazdunski's laboratory found 64 nanograms of tetrodotoxin per gram of zombie powder in only one of the six samples. A nanogram is one billionth of a gram. As even Hartung says: "If you asked me to drink 64 nanograms of tetrodotoxin, I would. It's not enough to do anything to a human."

Rivier recently told *Science* that he himself has now found between 5 and 20 micrograms of tetrodotoxin per gram of powder in one sample.

Why So Different?

What could possibly account for three laboratories finding such wildly different amounts of tetrodotoxin in the same sample? Rivier attributes the difference to the powder itself, which is both heterogeneous and very alkaline. Kao, in fact, maintains that the powder is so alkaline that tetrodotoxin would be "decomposed irreversibly into pharmacologically inactive products." The pH of the samples often exceeds 10, even after the powder is mixed with a buffered solvent. Yet Rivier and Davis contend that pH does not express itself in a dry powder. Says Rivier: "The fact that we have found after 3 years tetrodotoxin in powder kept at room temperature means that the powder itself is able to conserve tetrodotoxin for a long time." For his part, Davis reports that the bokors advised him to rub the powder onto the skin of his victim or place the powder in his shoes or to sprinkle the powder on the ground and whisper the victim's name. "The bokors never suggest that you put the powder in solution," says Davis.

Tetrodotoxin can cause an array of symptoms in lab animals, from wobbly legs to death. Blood pressure may drop and stay quite low. There is shallow breathing and wide paralysis. Without the aid of a respirator, Kao says, the animal usually dies. In cases of tetrodotoxin poisoning in humans, Bruce Halstead of the World Life Research Institute of Colton, California, reports that victims also suffer from decreased blood pressure. In Halstead's *Poisonous and Venomous Marine Animals of the World*, he states: "The muscles of the extremities become paralyzed and the patient is unable to move. As the end approaches the eyes of the victim become glassy. The victim may be comatose but in most cases retains consciousness, and the mental facilities remain acute until shortly before death."

In Japan, cases of fugu fish poisoning are not uncommon. About 100 people a year die from the delicacy. From the Japanese scientific literature and from newspaper accounts, Davis cites several cases of fugu fish poisoning where a victim lingers at the brink of death, but recovers. Says Kao: "If it happens, it is a very, very rare event."

Davis' Ballpark of Feasibility

The amount of tetrodotoxin necessary to produce the pharmacological effects that Davis attributes to zombification is unclear. Kao reports that 10 micrograms of pure tetrodotoxin per kilogram of body weight produces a lethal dose in 50% of the lab animals tested. According to the report from Lazdunski's laboratory in Nice, at 64 nanograms of tetrodotoxin per gram of crude poison, a bokor would have to administer 10 kilograms of powder to his victim to produce a lethal dose in 50% of his victims. Of course, the bokors are not trying to kill their victims, only to place them into a state resembling death. Using Rivier's latest figures, a bokor might only have to administer about 70 grams of poison or less. Kao reluctantly concedes that this "is getting into the ballpark of feasibility."

And it is through this window of feasibility that Davis presents his case. "It could well be that my hypothesis is in need of work or is incorrect, but it is not fraudulent," says Davis, who adds that because his critics approach his research as pharmacologists or toxicologists, they fail to appreciate the cultural context. The bokors can always rationalize their failures, says Davis. If a bokor overdoes it and kills a victim "too completely," no one is the wiser. It is a call from God. . . . While if a bokor fails to produce a state of near death, he can always try again. Davis notes: "The zombie powders are not manufactured by [a pharmaceutical company like] Merck Sharp & Dohme." Also, the puffer fish may harbor varying amounts of tetrodotoxin depending on the season and its sex.

Says Davis: "I've never maintained there is some kind of assembly line producing zombies in Haiti." He admits that it is, at best, a rare event. "I'm not even saying that it is happening today," says Davis.

Davis does indeed have his supporters. Harvard professor

Richard Evans Schultes, the grand old man of ethnobotany, calls his former student "a solid anthropologist and a good botanist and a very good field man with a promising future." As for Davis' hypothesis linking zombies to tetrodotoxin, Schultes says he did not scrutinize that aspect of the dissertation. "I don't know anything about the pharmacology of all this," says Schultes. Indeed, there were no pharmacologists or toxicologists on Davis' dissertation committee.

Irven DeVore, an anthropologist at Harvard who was on the committee, considers the Davis hypothesis "interesting but unproven." Like Schultes, DeVore judged the research as a work of anthropology, not pharmacology. "Red flags did not go up in my mind," says DeVore. "But if Davis has gone well beyond his data, he should have his wrist slapped."

As for paying for samples, this is a gray area. Anthropologists and field biologists often give mirrors, clothing, and sometimes cash to native people in exchange for information or assistance. Davis says that since Haitians are expected to pay for zombie powders, why shouldn't he?

The exhumation of the corpse, however, raises more troubling questions. Holmstedt calls the act "disgusting." Kao correctly points out that Davis did not just witness a grave-robbing, he commissioned it by paying a bokor to make zombie powder for him. The exhumation, though, does not bother Schultes: "I think they exhume people all the time. I don't see any problem there." Mark Plotkin, an ethnobotanist at the World Wildlife Fund and a former student of Schultes, says that Davis did not pay the bokor to exhume corpses, he paid for zombie powder.

DeVore, however, says that Kao might have a point. "I think the issue is whether Davis paid someone to do something he never does, or rarely does, or paid him to do something he routinely does," says DeVore. "There is a difference."

Says Timothy Plowman, an ethnobotanist at the Field

Museum in Chicago: "We're expected to participate in a lot of weird things in the field that we wouldn't do back home." DeVore adds that "anthropologists are forever witnessing something illegal." In his own research on the bushmen of the Kalahari, for example, DeVore says that "there is elephant poaching going on all around us."

Davis defends his actions in Haiti, saying that he simply played the role of participant-observer. In his interviews, Davis often mentions that his work has helped elevate voodoo from a folk cult to a legitimate religion in the minds of outsiders. Some of Davis' critics are not so sure. "Davis complains about the popular accounts of zombies, but here he has contributed to the very same thing," says Holmstedt. Desmangles of Trinity College says that the film made from Davis' book, complete with snakes crawling out of a zombie's mouth, "has taken us back 100 years."

For now, at least, the mystery of the zombies remains unsolved, despite all the noise and attention. For Davis, the zombie research might be over. It will at least have to wait until he finishes two other book projects that are occupying his time these days in Vancouver. Though Davis may make another trip to Haiti, he says he does not plan on becoming a "zombiologist." Says Davis: "My purpose was not to generate absolute truths." Kao agrees with that.

Epilogue: Analyzing the Evidence

In the 1850s a New Orleans businessman named J.B. Langrast publicly accused a local hairdresser and reputed "voodoo queen" named Marie Laveau of everything from robbery to murder. Shortly after, gris-gris (a voodoo term referring to fetishes or charms) began appearing on his doorstep in the form of roosters' heads, Langrast became progressively upset and finally fled New Orleans.

In the opinion of Raymond J. Martinez, Langrast was driven insane by the magical properties of the gris-gris and hexes placed on him by Laveau, whom he credits with telepathy in his book *Mysterious Marie Laveau*. Marie Laveau could only have flourished as she did, Martinez suggests, with the help of powerful voodoo spirits who held her in special favor.

Journalist Joe Nickell also researched the life of Marie Laveau and concluded that such deeds were explainable by less supernatural means. In Nickell's opinion, Laveau was a charlatan who used her natural talent for acquiring and exploiting useful gossip about prominent locals and pretended to do so by magical means. Nickell points out a complete lack of proof that Langrast was ever clinically insane. It was entirely possible, in Nickell's view, that Langrast's alleged flight was precipitated by very real fear of being killed by Marie Laveau's followers.

So who is right about Laveau—Martinez or Nickell? Not even scientists who have studied voodoo for years agree on how much reality lies behind the supernatural mystique.

However, readers can acquire insight to help shape their opinions on the topic by critically analyzing the evidence presented by experts, by those who have witnessed the effects of voodoo firsthand, and by voodoo's practitioners. The articles in this book provide various types of evidence and theories advanced in favor of the authors' viewpoints on voodoo. Some articles that sound equally reasonable directly contradict one another. It is up to the reader to determine which articles present a valid case for—or against—voodoo. This can be accomplished by reading the articles critically.

Reading critically does not mean that the reader should criticize the article by saying negative things about it. It means analyzing and evaluating what the author says, skeptically but with an open mind. This epilogue demonstrates how to develop a critical reading technique and apply it to examining the articles in this book.

The Author

One important factor in considering an article's position on voodoo is whether the author has any unique qualifications for writing about the topic. For instance, an article written by a biochemist who has used sophisticated equipment to test the contents of voodoo powders should be accorded more credibility than an article written by an adolescent member of a bizarre cult. Some authors are relating mere opinions or secondhand anecdotes from sources that are centuries old. Considering the authors' agendas and their backgrounds will give the reader a fresh perspective on their material.

Hypothetical Reasoning

Even when readers know nothing about the author of an article they can still evaluate the article on its own merits by using hypothetical reasoning. This is a scientific form of determining whether something makes sense, in this case whether the author has made a persuasive case for his or her claims. (Hypothetical reasoning should not be viewed as a clear-cut means of deciding the cold, hard truth of an author's claims, but it can help ascertain if the author has presented a reasonable case in support of those claims.)

Using hypothetical reasoning to analyze an article involves five steps:

1. State the author's claim (the hypothesis).
2. Gather the author's evidence supporting the claim.
3. Examine the author's evidence.
4. Consider alternative hypotheses or explanations.
5. Draw a conclusion about the author's claim.

Applying hypothetical reasoning to a pair of contradictory articles on voodoo may not decide once and for all whether voodoo magic is real, but it will help to discern the difference between strong arguments and weak ones and to judge which author has the best—or the most—evidence to support his or her claims.

In the following sections, hypothetical reasoning will be used to critically examine some of the articles in this book. Readers can practice applying the method to other articles.

State the Author's Claim (the Hypothesis)

A hypothesis is a statement that can be tested to determine the likelihood of its truth. To put it another way, it is not just an opinion but something that can be tested to determine whether it is true. Evaluating an article critically begins by stating the author's claim. Some authors may make more than one claim, but usually one main point predominates, summing up the article's position as a whole.

The following table shows the major claim of all but two articles in this book, reduced to a simple hypothesis.

Author	Hypothesis
Raymond J. Martinez	Marie Laveau was a voodoo queen.
Joe Nickell	Marie Laveau was a fraud.
Reginald Crosley	Voodoo's existence is corroborated by advanced physics.
Daniel Farson	
Michael White	Voodoo is not supernatural.
Wade Davis	Zombies are poison victims.
William Booth	
Roland Littlewood and Chavannes Douyon	Zombies are cases of mistaken identity.

One important thing to remember when writing a hypothesis is that it should be a statement that is clear, specific, and provable. The last hypothesis in the table above—"Zombies are cases of mistaken identity,"—may appear clear and specific, but both "zombies" and "mistaken identity" are vague terms. The wording could even imply that zombies are being mistaken for other supernatural zombies. Moreover, the article by Littlewood and Douyon focuses on only three cases of people whose zombiehood was disproven. A more specific hypothesis could be stated like this:

Roland Littlewood and Chavannes Douyon	Scientists found three alleged zombies to be mentally troubled people who had been mistaken for long-lost relatives or friends.

The hypotheses containing the word "voodoo" may also require more thought. Voodoo is a complex system of spiritual beliefs with many branches. New Orleans voodoo is not the same as Haitian voodoo to its followers, so broad declarations such as "voodoo is not supernatural" and "voodoo's existence is corroborated by advanced physics" may not suffice. Certainly Crosley and White would have wildly different notions about what is meant by the word *voodoo*.

Not every article has a provable hypothesis. The hypothesis "Marie Laveau was a voodoo queen" in the table for the article by Raymond J. Martinez is difficult to prove because Marie Laveau lived in the 1800s and anyone who witnessed her feats is long dead. Martinez can only offer his opinion and the oral testimonies handed down by unreliable sources. Many of the deeds ascribed to Laveau may have been exaggerated or fabricated or tailored to fit the folklore of the day because people found Laveau's style entertaining and wanted to believe in it. Martinez paints a portrait of a fascinating woman who led a life worth reading about, but it is hard to state that Marie Laveau's acts could only be accomplished by black magic as a provable hypothesis.

Some authors like Michael White make several claims in a single article. To examine the article critically, a hypothesis for each major claim needs to be stated.

Hypotheses are not stated for two articles in the table above. Read both articles and write a clear, specific, and (if possible) provable statement of each author's claim.

Gather the Author's Evidence Supporting the Claim

To test a hypothesis, the first step is to gather the evidence the author uses to support that hypothesis. The evidence is everything the author uses to prove that his or her claim is true. Sometimes a single sentence is a piece of evidence; on other occasions a string of paragraphs constitutes a single piece. In the last article in Chapter 1 Wade Davis offers the following evidence to back up his claim that zombies are people who have been poisoned:

1. Clairvius Narcisse and others remember being poisoned, revived, and enslaved on plantations.

2. Haitian *houngans* verified the existence of such a poison.
3. Wade Davis purchased a sample of the poison.
4. Tests on white rats showed that the poison would make a victim appear dead.
5. Wade Davis tracked down a sample of the reviving antidote and found it also viable.
6. Wade Davis discovered the existence of secret societies that employ zombie powder.
7. The zombie powder is found to contain tetrodotoxin, a chemical that causes people to appear dead.
8. Two scientists, Nathan S. Kline and Leon Roizin, verify Davis's chemical findings.

Examine the Evidence the Author Uses to Support the Claim

An author might use many types of evidence to support his or her claims. It is important to recognize different types of evidence and to evaluate whether they actually support the author's claims. Wade Davis's article uses four main forms of evidence: eyewitness and expert testimony, physical evidence, and statements of fact.

Eyewitness Testimony

Davis is not only the author of this article but also an eyewitness to the events he describes. His whole article is an example of eyewitness testimony (items 1, 2, 3, 5, 6, and 8). The right eyewitness can provide a great deal of anecdotal information about an event. However, this type of evidence cannot always be easily verified since it hinges largely on a person's memory of events. (This distinguishes it from hard evidence, which is usually something physical or measurable.) Sometimes people, even trained scientists, see what they want to see.

There is a common eyewitness memory experiment in

which a group of people is sitting in a classroom listening to a lecture or doing some other classroom activity. Suddenly a stranger bursts onto the scene. The stranger may "rob" one of the witnesses or do something else dramatic. Then the stranger leaves.

A few moments later, the instructor asks the students to tell what they witnessed. Invariably, different students remember different things. One remembers that the stranger was of average height and weight, another recalls that he was thin or heavy; one remembers that he had red hair, another remembers that a hood covered the stranger's head; one remembers that he was carrying a weapon, another remembers that his hands were empty; and so on. When something unexpected happens, especially when it happens quickly or evinces great emotion, the mind is not prepared to remember details. This is what makes the time frame Davis details an important aspect of his credibility. Davis is an experienced scientist who spent months accumulating evidence, exploring Haiti's back ways, and having chemicals analyzed, so his eyewitness testimony should be accorded more credibility than a visiting tourist with no technical background who made the same claims.

Another factor to consider in evaluating eyewitness articles is the witness's reputation. Does the witness (Davis, in this case) have a reputation for honesty? Publicity-seeking? Exaggeration? Flakiness? The William Booth article casts Davis as a glory hound who performed sloppy lab work—charges Davis vehemently disputes. Who is right?

For these reasons, independent corroborating witnesses can be important. Wade Davis did not conduct his research in a vacuum but worked in concert with other scientists he names, Nathan S. Kline and Leon Roizin, who corroborated his findings. This is an example of expert testimony (item 8), the use of knowledgable people or celebrities to support an assertion. Many television ads use expert testimony; for example, the GAP commercials that have popular entertainers singing while wearing GAP jeans, and commercials that have self-declared doctors praising aspirin and other medicines. Advertisers know that many people are influenced when a celebrity or expert says something is true.

Celebrity testimony usually does not have much value as evidence: If a celebrity wears a certain brand of jeans, does it mean the jeans are good quality? Hardly. It means the celebrity's agent got the celebrity some money to say the jeans are good.

Expert testimony can provide valuable evidence, however. Davis is himself an expert, and he cites respected scientists and eminent institutions by name. If these sources did not exist or did not support Davis's findings, William Booth would have been quick to point out these inconsistencies in his own article trying to debunk Davis. Davis mentions the consensus of chemists and pharmacologists, which is important: The experts must be expert on the topic under discussion, and the author must provide enough information to help the reader judge whether this person is a reliable source.

Physical Evidence

Physical evidence can be used to prove or disprove a hypothesis. In police cases, physical evidence includes fingerprints, DNA, murder weapons, and so on. In this article, physical evidence includes the white rats themselves cited in item 4, the poison powder that Davis claims to have purchased in item 3, and the antidote in item 5.

Statements of Fact

Items 4, 7, and 8 are statements of fact that present verifiable information—that is, they can be proven true (or false).

"Tests on white rats showed that the poison would make a victim appear dead"(item 4) is a statement of fact. The author states it as a fact, and it is a statement that is provable by investigation.

Ideally, to significantly support an author's claims, the statements of fact that he or she uses should be verifiable. They ought to be something that can be looked up in a book or the author should mention the source of the information so that the reader can confirm it. However, many authors expect readers to simply accept their statements of fact as true just because they say so. Be careful of accepting facts the author fails to substantiate. Look for corroborating evidence that helps confirm their truth.

Which of Davis's statements of fact can be verified from his article, and which cannot?

Consider Alternative Hypotheses

After examining the types of evidence the author has provided and considering how valuable the evidence is in supporting the author's claims, consider whether the author has presented other possible explanations. If the author considers only one explanation for the evidence, he or she may be presenting a biased view, or may not have fully considered the issue.

There are a few alternative explanations for Davis's thesis that zombies are poison victims but not supernatural in origin. One is that they are in fact reanimated corpses, a notion Davis never seriously considers. Another is that Narcisse and the other alleged zombies are lying or mentally ill. Still another possibility is that Davis himself is lying and manufactured the zombie powder to acquire fame and fortune.

It is the reader's job to decide if any of these scenarios are likelier than what the author is proposing.

Draw a Conclusion About the Author's Claim

Finally, after considering the evidence and alternative explanations, it is time to make a judgment, to decide whether the hypothesis makes sense. Readers can tally up the evidence that does and does not support the hypothesis and see how many pros and cons there are. But that is simplistic. Some evidence carries more weight than others. For instance, most of the evidence in Davis's article consists of eyewitness testimony that is hard to verify; the reader has to decide whether the author's account is accurate based on how credibly he presents his findings. Does Davis adequately support the claim that Clairvius Narcisse and others were poisoned using powder made from the venom of a poisonous fish and later dug from their graves?

Exploring Further

Now examine another article using hypothetical reasoning. In Michael White's article "Voodoo Is Real but Not Supernatural," perhaps the first thing worth noticing is that White comes to this subject with a bias against it. White is a former science editor for a British magazine and a consultant for the Discovery Channel series *The Science of the Impossible*. His article comes from a book in which he debunks various paranormal phenomena and tries to find scientific explanations for anything magic or supernatural. Thus, the reader must decide whether the author puts aside his bias and treats the subject as objectively as possible.

Review White's article using the steps for hypothetical reasoning.

State a Hypothesis

The effects of voodoo are not supernatural.

Gather the Author's Evidence

1. The fundamentals of voodoo "appear to be quite confused—a hodgepodge of different creeds and beliefs."
2. The author says voodoo "is claimed to be a mutual support system for what is a largely impoverished people."
3. Clairvius Narcisse and other "zombies" report being drugged but never dead.
4. Professor Roland Littlewood "claims that many zombies are actually mentally ill members of the community."
5. Hallucinogenic drugs are commonly used at voodoo rituals, inducing attendees to believe they are witnessing acts of magic.
6. Doctors in the 1920s discovered an overstimulation of the adrenal system that created an effect similar to the gradual "fading-away" described in mojo stories.

Examine the Evidence

In this article, White relies heavily on generalizations and statements of fact. He also uses statements of opinion, physical evidence, eyewitness testimony, and expert testimony.

Generalizations

A generalization is a broad conclusion based on a few examples. For instance, the statement "Beach vacations are great" is a generalization. In truth, beach vacations are not always great, depending on the weather, traveling companions, degree of sunburn, and other factors. Although generalizations can be true, they are based on inadequate evidence and can also be false.

Sometimes an author makes an implied generalization, naming one or two examples that lead the reader to generalize. In item 3, for example, the author mentions Clairvius Narcisse by name but no one else. The author wants the reader to generalize that the Narcisse case was typical of every other zombie report.

Generalizations are sometimes true, but without sufficient evidence to back them up, they do not prove much. Be aware of what evidence lies behind a generalization.

Does item 6 also qualify as an implied generalization? Decide if it is justified.

Statements of Fact

Review the section about statements of fact in the section of this epilogue that discusses Wade Davis's article. Then look at items 1, 2, and 6 and decide if any of these statements could qualify as statements of fact.

Eyewitness Testimony

Review the information on eyewitness testimony in the section on Davis's article. Then look at item 3. Does the Narcisse story lend credible support for White's hypothesis?

Expert Testimony

Does a generalization from an expert discussing his field of research (item 4) carry more weight than broad statements White makes without naming the sources of his information?

Consider Alternative Hypotheses

Does White consider alternative hypotheses? Does he consider explanations for his evidence that voodoo is not supernatural? Are there alternative hypotheses he should have considered?

Draw a Conclusion

Does Michael White make a good case for voodoo being real but not supernatural? What evidence most influences your decision?

Other Kinds of Evidence

Authors commonly use other types of evidence to support their claims. One important type of evidence is logical thinking, or logical argument. *Logic* comes from the Greek word for "reason." Logical thinking means to reason things out. (Hypothetical reasoning is a form of logical thinking.) A logical fallacy is when a person's reasoning seems to be logical but is not. For example, an overgeneralization such as "I have never seen anyone die of a voodoo curse, therefore it has never happened" may appear to be logical, but it is not. There are a lot of things a person may not have experienced that are real—for instance, spaceflight, the bubonic plague, or death—yet all exist.

Another kind of logical fallacy is a false analogy: wrongly comparing two things based on a common quality. Here is an example:

Honey bees make honey. Honey bees have yellow stripes.

Wasps also have yellow stripes, so wasps must make honey.

The fallacy is that honey making has nothing to do with yellow stripes, so the argument falls apart. Here is another example of a logical fallacy:

My dog seems to sense when I will be home from school.

My neighbor's dog also senses when its owner will be home from school.

Therefore, all dogs sense when their owners will be home from school.

The fallacy here is that the sample is too small. There are

millions of dogs in the world, and only two of them are in this sample. This is far too few to base such a broad generalization on.

A reader must carefully examine the author's logical thinking.

Now You Do It!

Choose one article from this book that has not already been analyzed and use hypothetical reasoning to determine if the author's evidence supports the hypothesis.

Name of article_____ Author_____

1. State the author's hypothesis.

2. List the evidence.

3. Examine the evidence. For each item you have listed under number 2, state what type of evidence it is (statement of fact, eyewitness testimony, etc.) and evaluate it: Does it appear to be valid evidence? Does it appear to support the author's hypothesis?

4. Consider alternative hypotheses. What alternative hypotheses does the author consider? Does he or she consider them fairly? If the author rejects them, does the rejection seem reasonable? Are there other alternative explanations you believe should be considered? Explain.

5. Draw a conclusion about the hypothesis. Does the author adequately support his or her claim? Do you believe the author's hypothesis stands up? Explain.

For Further Research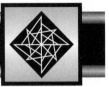

Books

Karen McCarthy Brown, *Mama Lola: A Voodoo Priestess in Brooklyn*. Berkeley: University of California Press, 1991.

Barbara Christensen, *The Magic and Meaning of Voodoo*. Milwaukee: Raintree Books, 1977.

Reginald Crosley, *The Vodou Quantum Leap: Alternate Realities, Power and Mysticism*. St. Paul, MN: Llewellyn, 2000.

Rod Davis, *American Vodou: Journey into a Hidden World*. Denton: University of North Texas Press, 1998.

Wade Davis, *Passage of Darkness: The Ethnobiology of the Haitian Zombie*. Chapel Hill: University of North Carolina Press, 1988.

———, *The Serpent and the Rainbow*. New York: Warner Books, 1985.

Migene Gonzalez-Whippler, *The Santeria Experience*. Englewood Cliffs, NJ: Prentice-Hall, 1982.

Jim Haskins, *Voodoo & Hoodoo: Their Tradition and Craft as Revealed by Actual Practitioners*. Chelsea, MI: Scarborough House, 1990.

Raymond J. Martinez, *Mysterious Marie Laveau*. New Orleans: Hope, 1956.

Alfred Mètraux, *Voodoo in Haiti*. New York: Schocken Books, 1959.

Joseph M. Murphy, *Santeria: An African Religion in America*. Boston: Beacon Books, 1988.

Milo Rigaud, *Secrets of Voodoo*. San Francisco: City Lights Books, 1985.

William B. Seabrook, *The Magic Island*. Whitefish, MT: Kessinger, 2003.

Robert Tallant, *Voodoo in New Orleans*. New York: Macmillan, 1962.

Luisah Teish, *Jambalaya*. New York: Harper & Row, 1985.

E. Fuller Torrey, *Witchdoctors and Psychiatrists: The Common Roots of Psychotherapy and Its Future*. New York: Harper & Row, 1986.

Michael White, *Weird Science: An Expert Explains Ghosts, Voodoo, the UFO Conspiracy, and Other Paranormal Phenomena*. New York: Avon Books, 1999.

Joseph J. Williams, *Voodoos and Obeahs*. New York: AMS, 1932.

Periodicals

William Booth, "Voodoo Science," *Science*, April 15, 1988.

Carole Devillers, "Haiti's Voodoo Pilgrimages of Spirits and Saints," *National Geographic*, March 1985.

Marvin Harris, "Death by Voodoo," *Psychology Today*, May 1984.

Nick Jordan, "What's in a Zombie?" *Psychology Today*, May 1984.

Joseph Nickell, "Voodoo in New Orleans," *Skeptical Inquirer*, January/February 2002.

Louis Saas, "Voodoo Therapy," *Vogue*, September 1986.

Web Sites

Sacred Arts of Haitian Vodou, www.amnh.org/exhibitions/ vodou. The American Museum of Natural History hosted this famous traveling exhibit from October 1998 to January 1999. This online companion offers detailed analysis of over five hundred Haitian voodoo relics along with general information about Haiti and its culture.

Santeria, www.religioustolerance.org/santeri.htm. Religious Tolerance.org offers glossaries on Santeria terminology and beliefs, along with statistics on the number and locations of Santeria followers worldwide.

The Vodou Page, http://members.aol.com/racine125/index.html. This Web site offers lessons in conducting voodoo rites, a detailed overview of the Haitian spirit world, and numerous articles ranging in topics from voodoo's role in Haitian politics to advanced herbology.

Index

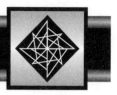

140